HOW TO PASS

STANDARD GRADE

HISTORY

John Kerr

HODDER
GIBSON
AN HACHETTE UK COMPANY

Acknowledgements

The Publishers would like to thank the following for permission to reproduce copyright material:
The introductory instructions and list of contents from the 2004 Standard Grade History General Level exam paper are reproduced with the permission of the Scottish Qualifications Authority.

Photo credits

Page 22 © The Print Collector/Alamy; page 86 © NI Syndication; page 122 © INTERFOTO Pressebildagentur/Alamy; page 130 Reprinted with permission from the **February 5, 1936** issue of *The Nation* magazine.
For subscription information, call 1-800-333-8536. Portions of each week's Nation magazine can be accessed at http://www.thenation.com.

Every effort has been made to trace all copyright holders, but if any have been inadvertently overlooked the Publishers will be pleased to make the necessary arrangements at the first opportunity.

Although every effort has been made to ensure that website addresses are correct at time of going to press, Hodder Gibson cannot be held responsible for the content of any website mentioned in this book. It is sometimes possible to find a relocated web page by typing in the address of the home page for a website in the URL window of your browser.

Hachette's policy is to use papers that are natural, renewable and recyclable products and made from wood grown in sustainable forests. The logging and manufacturing processes are expected to conform to the environmental regulations of the country of origin.

Orders: please contact Bookpoint Ltd, 130 Milton Park, Abingdon, Oxon OX14 4SB. Telephone: (44) 01235 827720. Fax: (44) 01235 400454. Lines are open 9.00–5.00, Monday to Saturday, with a 24-hour message answering service. Visit our website at www.hoddereducation.co.uk. Hodder Gibson can be contacted direct on: Tel: 0141 848 1609; Fax: 0141 889 6315; email: hoddergibson@hodder.co.uk

© **John Kerr 2005, 2009**
First published in 2005 by
Hodder Gibson, an imprint of Hodder Education,
an Hachette UK Company,
2a Christie Street
Paisley PA1 1NB

This colour edition first published 2009

Impression number   5 4 3 2
Year   2012   2011   2010

Cover photo © Garry Gay/Stone/Getty Images
Cartoons © Moira Munro 2005, 2008
Artwork by Peters and Zabransky
Typeset in 10.5 on 14pt Frutiger Light by Phoenix Photosetting, Chatham, Kent
Printed in Italy

A catalogue record for this title is available from the British Library

ISBN-13: 978 0340 973 899

CONTENTS

Contents

INTRODUCTION: HOW TO LEARN AND WHAT TO LEARN

This revision book will help you to achieve your best possible result in the Standard Grade History examination by telling you all you need to know about the exam. It tells you how to learn and what to learn and provides lots of practice for Knowledge and Understanding and Enquiry Skills questions. It even gives you the answers! By working your way through this book you will find it easier to answer exam questions and, in the process, gather valuable extra information about the exam topics.

How to Learn

Two years is a long time to prepare for anything. That is probably how long you have been doing your Standard Grade History course, so it makes sense to get the best possible result you can. This book will help you to do that.

For a start, there is no need to get bogged down in all sorts of technical jargon about different types of questions. After all, there is almost no choice in the Standard Grade exam.

Hints and Tips

Give your brain a chance!

Everyone learns in different ways and you might have heard of the phrase 'learning styles'. You will not learn effectively if you are learning because someone told you to or if you are thinking of doing something else or if you have recently had an argument.

Very few people learn best while sitting at a desk. Choose the place you work best in and find a time when you want to learn.

Do you have the self discipline to organise your learning? Of course you do, otherwise there would be no point starting! But choose a time when you feel positive about learning and when you want to do some revision. Even a small amount is better than nothing. A positive attitude will really help anyone's ability to learn.

Hints and Tips

Here are some tips on how to revise.

How do you know what to revise?

Your brain works best when it has a definite puzzle to solve, so try this.

Step 1: Decide on a focused topic or question to revise. That means a particular amount of knowledge for one revision session. For example, 'Why did the population in Scotland change between 1830 and 1930?'

Step 2: BEFORE you revise anything on the topic write a list of all that you already know about it. It might be quite a long list but you only need to write it once – and you now have a list of what you DO know about the topic in your long-term memory.

Step 3: Now do your revision – and this time you have a purpose. You are now looking for new information. When you have finished this session of revision write a new list of the new information you have learned.

Step 4: Now colour each list a different colour, for example, green for your first list with things you already knew and yellow for your list of new information. The use of colour will make each list easier to see in your mind's eye when you try to remember it.

Step 5: A day after you revise the topic try to remember as much as you can from the new yellow list. That's the information that was new to you so you need to reinforce your memory of that information. Try to visualise the yellow list and think what you wrote in it.

Step 6: Now look back again at the yellow list to remind you what you actually wrote. What had you forgotten? Write out the forgotten information again and this time shade it a different colour. When you return to revise that topic, try to remember what you wrote in the 'forgotten list' and the yellow list. Each time you do this routine you will reinforce your learning.

Hints and Tips

More ideas!

Step 1: When you have done no more than five minutes of revision STOP!

Step 2: Write a heading which sums up the topic you have been revising.

Step 3: Write a summary in no more than two sentences of what you have revised. Do not fool yourself. If you cannot do it or do not want to do it, why not? Do not ever say to yourself, 'I know it but I cannot put it into words.' That just means you do not know it well enough.

Hints and Tips

Use technology!

Why should everything be written down? Have you thought about 'mental' maps, diagrams, cartoons and colour to help you learn? And rather than write down notes, why not record your revision material onto mini disc or CDs or video? Why not make a video diary where you tell the camera what you are doing, what you think you have learned and what you still have to do. You could share these things with your friends. They deserve a laugh. Nobody said revision had to be boring. And after you gain the results you want you can watch the videos again and wonder why you got so stressed in the first place!

On the front page of your exam booklet you will see all the units and contexts listed, just like the example from a real past paper on the following page. Beside the unit and context names are page numbers. Turn to the correct page for your first context and get started.

1540/402

| NATIONAL QUALIFICATIONS 2004 | WEDNESDAY, 12 MAY 10.20 AM – 11.50 AM | HISTORY STANDARD GRADE General Level |

Answer questions from Unit I **and** Unit II **and** Unit III.

Choose only **one** Context from each Unit and answer Sections A **and** B. The Contexts chosen should be those you have studied.

The Contexts in each Unit are:

Use the information in the sources, and your own knowledge, to answer the questions.

Number the questions as shown in the question paper.

Some sources have been adapted or translated.

What You Should Know

It's vital to use time effectively.

At General Level you have 1 hour 30 minutes to do roughly 14 or 15 questions.

◆ You have half an hour for each unit.

◆ Each section might have a slightly different number of questions so do your sums and work out how long you can spend on each question.

◆ It's really important to try to finish the exam paper.

At Credit Level you will have 1 hour 45 minutes for the three units.

◆ You have 15 minutes more than at General but there is more to read.

◆ In one of the contexts you answer there will be an 8 mark question that asks you to 'write a short essay of several paragraphs'. Don't worry. The 8 mark question replaces two four mark questions!

What You Should Know

Doing the 8 mark short essay

◆ You MUST have a clear structure in your short essay. That means you must have an introduction, a middle section where you develop your ideas in the introduction, and then a conclusion.

◆ Start with a short introduction which lists the main points you will expand later in your answer.

◆ Develop each of the other points in your introduction by including as much relevant factual knowledge as you can.

◆ In your conclusion make sure you sum up your main points and make an overall answer which links directly to the main question you were asked.

◆ **But be careful**: Only spend about 10–12 minutes on the whole question. After all, it is only worth double the questions that you are allowing five minutes for.

What are KU and ES Questions?

Whatever level you sit, there will be Knowledge and Understanding **(KU)** questions and Enquiry Skills **(ES)** questions.

What You Should Know

KU

General level

KU questions have a source and then a question.

Look at the number of marks. If there are 3 marks you'll earn two marks by using the information in the source and the other mark will be given for relevant information from your own knowledge.

If there are 4 marks then it's three from the source and one point from your own knowledge.

Credit level

KU questions have no sources to start you off.

Revise for these question by preparing for the 'big questions' from the units you have studied.

What you should know continued ➢

What You Should Know continued

These big questions can be summed up as:

1) Why did events happen?

2) What were the main facts in the events you are revising?

3) What were the results of the events?

Another thing to remember is the difference between the words 'describe' and 'explain'.

'Describe' means tell the detailed factual story about the subject you are asked about. 'Explain' means give reasons why something happened or what the effects of an events were.

What You Should Know

ES

Enquiry Skills ask you to judge, or evaluate, sources.

Remember that information about a source starts from the information BEFORE the source itself, about:

- where the source comes from
- when it was produced and
- whether it is primary or secondary.

Think about how you should mention these points in your answer.

In any **ES** answer try to think how you could *include comments about who wrote the source* or *when it was written or* if it is *biased* or *neutral* or if it gives *fact* or *opinion*. These are all things you should consider when judging a source, so try to work such comments in to your answer.

Anything in your **ES** answers which shows that you are *judging a source* and *supporting your comments with evidence* is much better than just describing the source.

Hints and Tips

Sometimes people are confused by the way questions are asked. Phrases such as 'How valuable is Source A?', 'How reliable is Source C?' or 'How far does Source E . . .?' can be tricky unless you are prepared for them.

Try to have a style of answering these questions but remember it is never enough just to describe what the source says or shows. You are asked to write what you THINK about the source, not report what is in it.

Do yourself a favour by starting answers to these questions by saying they are PARTLY useful or reliable or whatever the question asked. That means you can give reasons why the sources are useful, such as it was written by an eyewitness, it was relevant, or, showed how people felt. But it also allows you to include ideas about why the source might NOT be fully useful, such as it only gives information about one city and not the whole of Scotland or only one person's point of view.

Remember

Remember that a biased source is always useful in some way. It might not give the whole picture about something but it reveals how people felt at the time. If you do say a source is biased remember to quote a short part of the source which shows the bias otherwise a marker will think you are just guessing.

Think also if the information in a source matches up with your own knowledge. Be brave enough to write that a source might only be of limited use since it does not contain all the information that it could.

You might get a question based on a cartoon or photograph:

◆ What is the picture about?

◆ What do any words in the picture or cartoon mean?

◆ Are the words making a joke about the picture or do they maybe mean the opposite of what they seem to say?

Try to explain what all the people or things in the cartoon mean and how they are relevant to the question.

You are also very likely to be asked to compare sources.

Remember continued ➤

Remember *continued*

The best way to do this is to compare the sources point by point. For example, if you were comparing two people you would not describe each person separately. You would compare their hair, size, clothes, shoes, facial expression and so on. The same is true of the sources. Do not just describe one source and then the other.

Instead go from one point in one source to a connected point in the other source and compare the points of view of the writers. Do that all the way through the sources. If they differ write something like 'the sources take a different point of view about .... because on one hand Source A says .... but on the other hand Source B says ......'. You will find examples of comparison questions later in this book.

What You Should Know

The 'mini investigation'

The Issue

In the Enquiry Skills section of Changing Life in Scotland and Britain, you will find a sub heading 'The issue for investigation is ...' and then a box with a statement inside it. This statement is called the **issue** and it will **NOT** be a question. It will be a **statement** and you have to use the sources and your own knowledge to deal with the three questions which are part of the mini investigation. There are examples of mini investigations in the Changing Scotland section of this book.

At **General** Level you will be given two sources and three questions to accompany the issue. The style of questions is the same every year.

At **Credit** Level you will be given **THREE sources** and **three questions** to accompany the issue. The style of questions is the same every year.

Hints and Tips

There are, of course, certain ways of answering the different types of question in the 'mini investigation'.

The first 'mini investigation' question will ask you to evaluate a source.

Use the ideas about answering **ES** questions already mentioned in this book to help you.

The second mini investigation question can be tricky, so make it easy for yourself. The question will ask you to decide what evidence supports the original issue and what evidence does not support the idea. You are being asked to **select and organise** the information you have about the main issue, so all you have to do is write down brief extracts from the sources once you have decided what evidence is for or against the issue. You don't have to make any comment about them in this question. Just use *the exact words*.

The third question in the mini investigation questions asks for a conclusion and you **MUST** follow instructions here.

To answer the conclusion successfully:

◆ You must decide whether or not you agree with the statement at the beginning of the mini investigation.

◆ You must quote evidence from the sources to support your decision.

◆ You MUST include information 'from your own knowledge' – that means details NOT in the sources that are relevant and support your decision.

UNIT 1 CONTEXT B: CHANGING SCOTLAND AND BRITAIN 1830–1930

Population Change

What You Should Know

Population growth and distribution

Between 1830 and 1930 the population of Scotland and Britain increased from about 16 million to 45 million.

The distribution of population also changed. The population of Britain became urbanised. That means fewer people lived in the countryside and more lived in towns and cities.

The biggest movement of people was from the Highlands of Scotland and away from Ireland.

You do not have to know about the Highland Clearances in detail but you should be aware that many Highlanders were forced to move from their homes to make way for sheep farms which earned more money for the lairds. Many Highland people moved to new villages in the Highlands or to the industrial towns of central Scotland or England. Others chose to leave Britain and start a new life abroad, often in Canada, Australia or New Zealand.

You must be able to *describe examples of push and pull reasons*. A *push reason* means they were *forced to go* and *pull reasons* means people *wanted to move* for attractive reasons.

In the case of Ireland, the potato famine of the 1840s caused widespread starvation and thousands of Irish people migrated to Britain or the USA. Irish migration continued throughout the 19th and 20th centuries. Irish labourers were vital in helping to build Britain's railways and many other industries. Local Scots were often resentful of the Irish newcomers who worked for lower wages and were usually Catholics moving into mainly Protestant Central Scotland.

You should be able to describe the type of jobs done by Irish migrants and also the economic and social effects of Irish migration to central Scotland.

Questions *and* Answers

Population Change – Credit

KU Q Between 1830 and 1930 a rising birth rate led to an increase in population.

How important a factor was a rising birth rate in explaining population growth between 1830 and 1930? *(4 marks)*

KU

The rising birth rate was one reason for increased population but you must also include and explain the importance of at least three of the following:

◆ the falling death rate

◆ better diet

◆ improving health and hygiene

◆ earlier marriages

◆ improving living conditions

◆ immigration.

ES Q **The issue for investigating is:** People were forced to leave the highlands of Scotland against their wishes.

In *Source A*, a journalist describes how people left Scotland for Australia in 1853:

'His Royal Highness Prince Albert has become Patron of the Highland and Island Emigration Society. Since the end of May 1852, the society has sent 30,000 people to Australia. H.M.S. Hercules is now in the harbour of Campbeltown, taking immigrants on board to aid the relief of hardship in Britain caused by the surplus of population. At the same time, this action will help the relief of distress in Australia caused by short supply of labourers. Some emigrants are pleased to know that land and jobs await them.'

Source B is taken from Highland Change by A F Kerr, published in 1989.

'Many highland landlords are still remembered for their role in this disgraceful episode in Scottish history. Some went as far as to order their managers to set fire to the houses of the crofters in remote areas like Sutherland in order to force them to leave their crofts and make way for more profitable ways of farming. The people did not want to go and had to be dragged out of their homes so that the crofts could be destroyed.'

HOW TO PASS STANDARD GRADE HISTORY

Source C is taken from the diary of a Church of Scotland minister in Paisley, near Glasgow, in 1856:

'In spite of the overcrowding and poor housing, there has been a considerable increase in the population of the parishes of Paisley and other lowland towns. People have moved into the district attracted by the promise of employment in the many mills which are flourishing in the district. Many of these incomers are the homeless Highlanders of Scotland or the starving Irish.'

Q 1 How valuable is *Source A* for investigating the reasons for Scottish population migration in the nineteenth century? *(4 marks)*

Q 2 What evidence in the sources supports the view that people might be happy to leave their traditional way of life?

What evidence in the sources suggests that people were unhappy to leave their traditional way of life? *(6 marks)*

Q 3 Is it true to say that people were forced to leave the Highlands of Scotland against their wishes? Use evidence from the sources and your own knowledge to reach a balanced conclusion. *(5 marks)*

ES

A 1 You must evaluate *Source A* – that means judge its importance – as a source of information and evidence about emigration from Scotland. **You should include and explain the following points:**

◆ It is an eyewitness report from the time, a primary source.

◆ The journalist gives objective, detailed information.

◆ The information is relevant to the subject of emigration from Scotland.

◆ The writer is not emotionally involved in the emigration and takes a positive viewpoint that emigration is helping the situation.

◆ The source suggests both negative and positive reasons for emigration. While some were being 'sent', possibly against their will, others were attracted by the possibility of a new life overseas.

◆ Overall the source is of limited value since it does not give a full explanation of migration from Scotland between 1830 and 1930.

Questions *and* Answers *continued*

A 2   First of all you should use evidence from the sources which supports the issue:

From Source A

'people were sent' which suggests they did not choose to go.

'taking emigrants on board to aid the relief of hardship in Britain caused by the surplus of population' suggests that people were pushed into leaving by overcrowding.

From Source B

managers were ordered 'to set fire to the houses of the crofters ... to force them to leave'

'The people did not want to go and had to be dragged out of their homes'

From Source C

'Many of these incomers are the homeless Highlanders'.

You must also remember to deal with the other part of the question and select evidence which does not support the issue:

From Source A

'Some emigrants are pleased to know that land and jobs await them' in Australia.

From Source B

There is no evidence which does not support the issue here.

From Source C

'People have moved into the district attracted by the promise of employment ... Many of these incomers are the ... Highlanders of Scotland'.

A 3   In this answer you must provide a balanced conclusion. This means you must weigh up the evidence from all three sources and sum up the reasons which support the issue, the points which do not support the issue and then write down whether or not you agree with the issue. *You must also include some of your own information here. If you do not you will only get about half marks.*

You should write that many highlanders moved for both push and pull reasons. While many were forced to move as a result of overpopulation, hunger or the actions of the landlords, others moved for more positive reasons such as the attractions of a new life overseas and job prospects in towns and cities in Scotland.

Questions *and* Answers *continued*

From your own knowledge you could mention:

The introduction of sheep farming and the social change in the Highlands which caused Highland chiefs no longer to see their tenants as fighting men but as obstacles in the way of making money by producing meat and wool for the growing lowland population.

On the other hand you could develop more positive reasons for moving such as the attraction of better pay elsewhere and also that landlords sometimes provided new homes on the coast or paid the travelling costs of people who wanted to migrate.

Health and Housing

What You Should Know

In the nineteenth century the movement of population from the countryside to the towns caused health and housing problems. Most of these problems were linked to overcrowding. Over 30% of families had only one small room for everyone to eat, sleep and live in. Most families had between 5 and 12 people.

In Scottish towns more than half the population lived in cramped rooms in tenements which were four or five storey blocks of flats. The worst tenements were called 'slums'.

In the countryside things were little better. Rural cottages, or black houses in the highlands, usually had rough, low stone walls, earth floors with turf or thatched roofs. These had no water supply or sanitation. Animals were often in the same room as people. To make matters worse most farm workers lived in tied houses which meant the house came with the job. A family which became unemployed also lost its home.

If a question asks about housing conditions in Scotland, you should be able to describe housing conditions in the towns AND the countryside in both the Lowlands and the Highlands and Islands.

What You Should Know

In the 19th century slum areas of towns and cities were very unhealthy places where diseases could spread easily. The main illnesses were cholera, typhoid, typhus and tuberculosis (TB). Poor diet and bad working and living conditions were the main reasons for ill health.

By the middle of the 19th century doctors were starting to link bad housing and lack of fresh water to the spread of diseases. Slowly, new medical improvements, better housing, improved diet, drains and clean water improved the health of people in towns and cities.

Bad housing existed through all the 19th century and well into the 20th century but, remember, it was not like this for everyone all the time.

The rich and the middle classes lived in well built tenements and the even wealthier lived in villas – large houses surrounded by large gardens.

Be able to give a balanced description of town conditions in the 19th century. It was not all slums and disease!

Remember

By the end of the 19th century it was clear that slums would have to be knocked down and new, better houses built. After the First World War (1914–1918) the government promised to build many new houses.

You should know about the housing acts which led to more council houses being built such as the Addison Act, the Wheatley Act and the Greenwood Act.

You should be able to explain how the new council estates were better than the old slums.

You should also be able to explain why some people did not like living in the new housing estates.

By 1930 health and housing for most people was better than it had been in 1830.

You should be able to describe the main differences in town life between 1830 and 1930.

Questions *and* Answers

Health and Housing – General

This source describes problems caused by a lack of clean water in the 19th century:

'**Typhus, carried by lice from unwashed bodies, killed many people in the slums. Typhoid fever and cholera also resulted from dirty food or contaminated (polluted) water. The terrifying cholera epidemics, such as those of 1831–1832 and 1849, killed over 100,000 people.**'

KU Q How important for people's health was a clean water supply in the 19th century? *(4 marks)*

KU

◆ A clean water supply was important.

◆ Typhus was carried by lice from unwashed bodies.

◆ Typhoid fever and cholera resulted from dirty (unwashed) food.

◆ Typhoid and cholera were also spread by polluted water.

◆ These diseases killed people.

◆ Lack of water allowed epidemics to spread, killing over 100,000 people.

From your own knowledge you could mention:

Disease started to decline with the arrival of clean piped water in cities. Flush toilets and sewerage took away waste.

Clean drinking water stopped dehydration of the sick.

Plentiful clean tap water to wash improved personal hygiene.

ES Q The issue for investigating is:

Doctors were unaware that bad living conditions caused illness in 19th century Scotland.

Source A is from a report by Dr. Keith of Edinburgh. It was written in 1838.

'**Many of the diseases from which the poor suffer, especially cholera, are caused by the filthy conditions in which they live. We must clean up our cities. These diseases could be prevented by clearing away the rubbish, providing proper water supplies and better ventilation**'.

Questions and Answers continued

Source B is a report by Dr. Andrews of Glasgow. It was written in 1840.

'Cholera broke out in February and lasted until July. Most of the dead had worked in the local cotton mills. It is my belief that the heat and the noise in factories and cotton dust in the lungs of the workers cause diseases to spread. I can offer no help to the sick who ask for help. They must work in the factories, so they will catch the diseases.'

Q 1   How useful is *Source A* about the effects of bad living conditions on health?   *(3 marks)*

Q 2   What evidence is there in *Source A* that doctors were aware that bad living conditions caused diseases?

What evidence is there in *Source B* that doctors were unaware that bad living conditions caused diseases?   *(5 marks)*

Q 3   How far were doctors unaware that bad living conditions caused diseases? Use evidence from the sources and your own knowledge to come to a conclusion.   *(4 marks)*

ES

A 1   When answering question one the following points would earn you marks:

It is a primary source from 1838 about health and housing and, therefore, it is relevant to the issue and to the study period. ***Remember at General Level it is never enough just to say a source is primary or secondary.*** Always develop that comment by saying why that is significant. For example, it is written by a doctor, therefore, the content is likely to be appropriate and informed.

◆   The source makes a direct link between housing and ill health.

◆   The source makes proposals to improve the situation.

◆   The source mentions cholera as a specific disease linked to living conditions.

◆   However, the source only focuses on 1838 so it may not typical of all of the 19th century.

◆   The source only focuses on Edinburgh so may not be typical of all of Scotland.

Questions and **Answers** continued

A 2 **First of all you should use evidence from the sources which support the issue:**

From Source A:

A direct link is made between housing and ill health – 'many of the diseases from which the poor suffer ... in which they live.'

The writer is aware that city wide cleaning is necessary – 'we must clean up our cities.'

The writer makes proposals to improve the situation – 'The diseases could be prevented by clearing away the rubbish, providing proper water supplies and better ventilation'.

From *Source B* you must identify evidence that doctors were unaware that bad living conditions caused diseases:

The doctor states, 'It is my belief that the heat and the noise in factories and cotton dust in the lungs of the workers cause diseases.'

The doctor implies that diseases are inevitable since: 'I can offer no help ... they must work in the factories so they will catch the diseases.'

A 3 **In this answer *you must reach a conclusion* and decide whether or not you agree** that doctors were unaware that bad living conditions caused illness in 19th century Scotland. You should make use of source evidence used in previous answers to present a balanced summary of the arguments. You must then use your own knowledge to develop your answer further, such as, lack of medical knowledge in the mid-19th century explains doctor B's attitude. It was not until 1850 that a clear link was established between polluted water and cholera as a result of research by Snow, Chadwick and Littlejohn.

Farming Changes

What You Should Know

You must know how and why farming changed and also what it was like to live and work as a farm labourer in the 19th century.

Between 1830 and 1930 new farming methods along with new technology made farming more efficient but as more and more machines arrived many workers lost their jobs.

You must be able to describe, with examples, new farming methods and new technology and describe how it made farming more efficient.

Be able to explain why fewer workers were needed on farms – clue: new technology.

Between the 1840s and the 1870s farming in Britain had a Golden Age. The Golden Age was the time when everything was going well for farm owners.

You should know some reasons why there was a Golden Age of farming but also that, for farm labourers, life was still hard.

You should also be able to describe examples of hard living and working conditions for farm workers.

The Golden Age stopped suddenly in the 1870s and bad times hit British farming. Reasons for the depression in farming included foreign competition, the use of new technology by foreign competitors and several years of cold wet summers in Britain.

You should know details of the foreign competition faced by British farmers such as what produce was sent to Britain, from where, and how new technology, such as canning, allowed such long distance competition.

By 1930 there were many fewer people working on farms and many more machines being used than in 1830. The working and living conditions of farm workers were, however, still hard.

Questions *and* Answers

Farming Changes – Credit

A few machines can do the work of many hands.

KU Q Give a brief account of changes in working conditions for farm workers between 1830 and 1930. *(4 marks)*

KU

You should mention:

◆ Long hours.

◆ Working in all weathers.

◆ Low wages.

◆ Workers often lived in tied houses.

◆ Workers often moved jobs, taking new jobs at feein' fairs.

◆ New technology such as threshing machines altered the way of working on the land.

◆ Alternative work was not always available.

◆ There was a fall in demand for older skills as mechanisation arrived, such as threshing machines, tractors and combined harvesters.

The use of young children, particularly in the gang system in areas of Britain, could also be mentioned.

ES Q The issue for investigating is:

New technology helped farmers and farm workers in Scotland in the 19th century.

Study the following three sources:

Source A is from a report by the minister of Stenton, East Lothian. It was written in 1835.

'I know the local farm workers very well and they are all distressed. While the new machines make big profits for the lairds*, the workers see only hunger and unemployment ahead of them. The new machines do their jobs faster and cheaper than any one person can do. Is it any wonder that a laird would rather spend money on his machines than on his people?'

*laird – a Scots word for a landowner

Questions and Answers *continued*

Source B is from evidence given by a young woman who worked on a borders farm in 1860:

'I have worked since I was five years old. I'm now sixteen. Machines can't do all the jobs on a farm. We spend weeks in the fields pulling and cutting turnips and picking potatoes. My back aches, my ankles swell and tears run down my face. We are made to work in all weathers. My sister died of the cold last year. If we complain we get beaten and worse.'

Source C is from *Farming Changes* published in 1987:

'For many farms new technology was a wonderful thing. Farms became more efficient and undoubtedly without the new machines the farms would not have been able to supply the growing towns with food. There were large profits to be made in the Golden Age. However, for the farm workers it was a different story. Mechanisation did not destroy all jobs and it would also be wrong to think that machines appeared all over Scotland on farms at the same time. At the same time there was a steady drift of workers away from the countryside to the towns and who is to say that the worn out farm labourers did not find a better life in the towns?'

Q 1 How valuable is *Source A* for investigating the effect of new technology on the lives of farm workers in the 19th century?
(4 marks)

Q 2 What evidence in the sources supports the view that new technology helped farmers and farm workers in Scotland in the 19th century?

What evidence in the sources supports the view that new technology did **not** help farmers and farm workers in Scotland in the 19th century? *(6 marks)*

Q 3 How important do you think new technology was in changing the lives of farmers and farm workers in the 19th century? You should use evidence from the sources and your own knowledge to reach a balanced conclusion. *(5 marks)*

Questions and **Answers** continued

Figure 2.1 A cartoon published by *Punch* in 1863.

ES

New technology helped farmers and farm workers in Scotland in the 19th century.

A 1   You must evaluate *Source A* – that means judge its importance – as a source of information and evidence about whether or not new technology helped farmers and farm workers in Scotland in the 19th century.

From Source A you you could mention:

◆   It is a primary source relevant to the issue.

◆   It is an eye witness report from an informed source – 'I know local farm workers very well'.

◆   The writer is a 'neutral' observer – a church minister – not employed in farming.

◆   There is some bias in the harsh tone of the last sentence.

◆   The tone is very sympathetic to the farm workers and implies criticism of the lairds who make 'big profits'.

◆   The source only refers to the early 19th century and only south east Scotland so does not provide an overview in terms of either the time or the location asked about in the question.

The source does not suggest any positive gains from the use of new technology.

Questions and Answers continued

A 2   Remember there are two parts to this question:

You must select and organise evidence in the sources which *does* and *does not* support the issue that new technology helped farmers and farm workers.

In support of the issue you could mention:

From Source A

Big profits for lairds.

Jobs are done faster.

Jobs are completed more cheaply.

From Source B

No direct benefits are identified in source B.

From Source C

New technology is described as 'a wonderful thing'.

Farms became more efficient.

Farms could supply towns with food.

There was a 'Golden Age of farming' when farm owners did well.

Large profits were made.

Against the issue you could mention:

From Source A

Workers see only hunger ahead.

Workers see only unemployment ahead.

From Source B

Machines cannot do all the jobs on a farm.

Made to work in all weathers.

My back aches, my ankles swell and tears run down my face.

If we complain we get beaten and worse.

We spend weeks in the fields pulling and cutting turnips.

My sister died of the cold.

Questions *and* Answers *continued*

From Source C

New technology was a wonderful thing, but for the farm workers it was a different story.

Workers left farming and moved to cities.

A 3 **In this answer *you must reach a conclusion and decide whether or not you agree*** that new technology helped farmers and farm workers in Scotland in the 19th century.

You should make use of source evidence used in previous answers to present a balanced summary of the arguments. You must then use your own knowledge to develop your answer further such as:

◆ New technology was used abroad and led to an increase in foreign competition for farmers in Britain.

◆ New jobs were created by new technology such as machine maintenance.

◆ New businesses such as Ransomes employed people and specialised in making agricultural machinery.

◆ The move to cities may not have been bad for all workers who improved their lives.

◆ Food became cheaper as result of new technology which benefited workers.

◆ New technology did little to help the bad living conditions of farm labourers.

◆ New technology had little effect on the lives and work of highland and island communities and in small farms generally.

Coal Changes

What You Should Know

In the 19th century, changes in industry, housing and transport meant that more and more coal was needed. As a result, coal mines got bigger and deeper and coal mining became more dangerous.

You must be able to explain why more coal was needed and describe what dangers faced coal miners.

A miner's life was hard, dangerous and often short. Accidents and disease killed thousands. Miners also lived in villages near the pit. The pit village was owned by the mine owner. If a miner lost his job, his family lost their home.

What you should know continued ➤

What You Should Know continued

Before 1842 the word 'miner' meant any man, woman or child who worked down a pit. There were different types of jobs such as hewers, bearers, trappers and putters.

You must be able to describe what these jobs involved.

In 1842 a Mines Act was passed by the government. There were other laws passed later which also changed the rules about who could work in mines and how they could become safer.

Be able to describe how these new laws made mines safer and what rules were made about who could work in a mine.

To make coal mining safer and more efficient, mines had to change. New technology was used to make mines more efficient and safer.

Be ready to describe some examples of the new technology and explain how they made mines safer and more efficient.

Coal was still a very important industry at the beginning of the 20th century but by 1930 it was facing difficulties such as lack of investment in new technology, foreign competition and competition from new fuels.

Be able to explain what these three problems mean.

Questions and Answers

Coal Changes – General

> In *Source A* Mr I.D. Rhodes describes his concerns about the future of the coal industry in 1920:

'Germany and the USA flood our country with cheap coal and in our homes and factories electricity is the new power. Transport, too, is changing. If the railways decline, so will the need for our coal.'

KU Q   Describe the problems faced by the coal industry in Britain in 1920. *(3 marks)*

KU

You must include the following:

◆   Germany and the USA flood our country with cheap coal.

◆   Electricity is the new power.

◆   As railways decline, so will the need for our coal.

Questions *and* Answers *continued*

From your own knowledge you could mention:

Mine owners do not want to spend money on new, efficient cutting machines.

Many ships burned oil and not coal.

Steam trains are being replaced by cars and lorries.

ES Q   **The issue for investigating is:**

Working conditions in coal mines were bad in the 1840s.

Source A is from evidence given to government investigators finding out about working conditions in coal mines in 1841:

'My name is Jane Watson. I have worked underground for 33 years. I have nine children. Three of my babies were born down the mine but two of them were dead.

My work is dragging carts of coal with a metal chain round my belly. My children help me load the cart. I don't want them to work in the mine but I have no choice. I feel old and worn out although I am only 40 years old.'

Source B is from the Renfrew Review's report about an investigation into coal mines published in 1842:

'The Commission investigating conditions in the coal mines have described the terrible conditions in which men, women and children work in our coal mines. But is it the whole truth? The report made no mention of the Davey safety lamp which has reduced the risk of explosions or of many mine owners who provide schools for their children and pay money out of their own pocket to women who are expecting a baby and unable to work.'

Q 1   How useful is *Source A* about working conditions in coal mines in the 1840s?   *(3 marks)*

Q 2   What evidence is there in *Source A* that working conditions in coal mines were bad?

What evidence is there in *Source B* that working conditions in coal mines were not so bad?   *(5 marks)*

Q 3   To what extent were working conditions in coal mines in the 1840s bad? Use evidence from the sources and your own knowledge to come to a conclusion.   *(4 marks)*

Questions *and* Answers *continued*

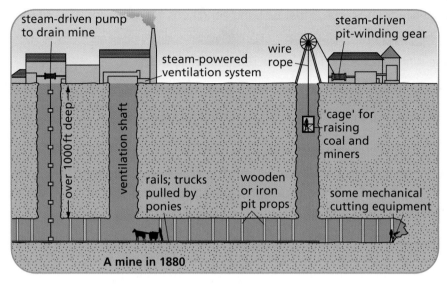

steam-driven pump to drain mine

steam-powered ventilation system

wire rope

steam-driven pit-winding gear

over 1000ft deep

ventilation shaft

'cage' for raising coal and miners

rails; trucks pulled by ponies

wooden or iron pit props

some mechanical cutting equipment

A mine in 1880

Figure 2.2 A mine in 1880

ES

Working conditions in coal mines were bad in the 1840s.

A 1   It is a primary source giving eye witness comments about working conditions in coal mines in 1841. *Remember at General Level it is never enough just to say a source is primary or secondary.* Always develop that comment by saying why that is significant.

◆   The source is by a government investigator finding out about working conditions in coal mines, therefore, it is likely to be unbiased.

◆   There is some detail of mine work.

◆   There is evidence of female work.

◆   The evidence given is from a mature woman with no obvious bias.

◆   However, the evidence is from only one person and no other opinion is included.

A 2   *From Source A* evidence that working conditions in coal mines were bad includes:

Pregnant women work in mines.

The work is hard with chains around workers bellies while they drag the coal.

Children working in mines.

A feeling of being 'worn out' by work.

Questions and Answers continued

Evidence from *Source B* that working conditions in coal mines were not too bad includes:

The writer claims the reports are not the whole truth.

The writer comments on new safety lamp, fewer explosions.

The writer comments on schools for children in some areas.

The writer comments on money paid to women while unable to work.

A 3   In this answer you must reach a conclusion and decide whether or not you agree with the issue that working conditions in coal mines were bad in the 1840s.

You should make use of source evidence used in previous answers to present a balanced summary of the arguments. You must then use your own knowledge to develop your answer further, such as the Government enquiry collected much evidence that conditions were bad in many mines. The positive side of coal mining was usually given by mine owners such as Lord Londonderry who tried to discredit the evidence given by children since it was in his interests to keep children working in coal mines as they were cheap to employ. Not all the evidence of harsh working conditions, however, came from children. It was also collected from adults and was probably more reliable.

Political Change and Votes for Women

What You Should Know

Between 1867 and 1928 Britain became more democratic which means that more people gained a say in how the country was governed. It also means the political system became fairer.

In 1867 and again in 1884 the rules about who could vote were changed, however, only 16% of men could vote after the 1867 change and only 29% of men could vote after 1884. And no women could vote at all!

The voting system was made fairer in 1872 when voting at elections could be done in secret and the total number of MPs was spread more fairly across the country with more MPs representing the busy towns and fewer coming from the less populated countryside.

Remember

You must understand what the words 'democracy' and 'democratic' mean and be able to use them in an answer.

You must be able to describe how the political system in Britain was unfair before 1867 and how it became fairer after that date.

You should be able to describe how Britain had become MORE democratic but also explain that by 1900 it was not yet a democratic country.

What You Should Know

Before 1918 women could not vote. In the 19th century many women were treated as second-class citizens. Many women were forced to work long hours for low wages in awful conditions. Even middle class women faced huge difficulties in their chosen careers. Put simply, women had no political voice so little was done to make their lives easier. That is why organisations were set up to give women the right to vote.

A word for the right to vote is 'suffrage' so when the National Union of Women's Suffrage Societies was set up they were nicknamed 'Suffragists'. Suffragists used peaceful methods at first such as speeches, meetings, marches, demonstrations, and petitions.

In 1903 another organisation was set up called the Women's Social and Political Union. They were called 'Suffragettes' and had the motto 'Deeds not words'. 'Deeds' means doing something, not just talking about it. At first they used peaceful methods but became more angry and militant as time passed and no changes happened. After 1910 Suffragette methods became more violent.

When the First World War broke out the Suffragettes' protest stopped and women took on many jobs previously done by men only. Women were also very important in munition factories making explosives and bullets for the war effort.

Remember

You must be able to explain the difference between Suffragists and Suffragettes.

You should be able to describe militant suffragette protests including hunger strikes.

You should be able to list many different 'men's jobs' done by women during the war.

What You Should Know

By 1918 most politicians were convinced that women had earned respect during the war and deserved the right to vote – so some women over 30 were given the right to vote, but these were not the munition girls who helped in the war effort. They had to wait until 1928 when all men and women were given the right to vote when they became 21.

Questions and Answers

Parliamentary Reform – Credit

Between 1867 and 1918 Britain became more democratic.

KU Q Give a brief description of how Britain became more democratic between 1867 and 1918. *(5 marks)*

KU

You could include in your answer:

- Men in towns gained the vote in 1867.
- Men in the countryside gained vote in 1884.
- Men over 21 and women over 30 gained the vote in 1918.
- The voting system also became fairer with:
- secret voting from 1872
- more equal sized constituencies
- less corruption at elections after the Corrupt and Illegal Practices Act of 1883.

All these changes helped Britain become more democratic.

ES Q   The issue for investigating is:

Women gained the vote because of the campaigns of the women's suffrage movement.

Source A is adapted from the book *Women and Change* by Angus Garrett, published in 1975:

'The formation of the National Union of Women's Suffrage Societies in 1897 was a major step forward for the cause of women's rights. Under the leadership of Millicent Fawcett, they organised peaceful demonstrations and public meetings in order to increase the pressure on the government for change.'

Source B is taken from a letter written by Mrs E. Moss to her friend in 1913:

'I still cannot understand why Emily felt it necessary to take such drastic action. We have had the attention of the press for some time and the campaign of civil disobedience and hunger strikes has made the government very unpopular. It is only a matter of time before Mr Asquith will give way to our demands for the same political rights as men.'

Source C is taken from a newspaper report published in a Glasgow newspaper in 1910:

'The Suffragette movement, under the leadership of Mrs Pankhurst, has done much to alienate members of the government who do not wish to be seen to be bullied into making concessions to a group of extremists in order to preserve civil order.'

Q 1   How valuable is *Source B* as evidence of the success of the women's suffrage movement?   *(4 marks)*

Q 2   What evidence in the sources supports the view that women gained the vote because of the success of the women's suffrage movement?

What evidence in the sources contradicts the view that women gained the vote because of the success of the women's suffrage movement?   *(6 marks)*

Q 3   To what extent was the women's suffrage movement responsible for women winning the right to vote? Use evidence from the sources and your own knowledge to reach a balanced conclusion. *(5 marks)*

UNIT 1 CONTEXT B: CHANGING SCOTLAND AND BRITAIN 1830–1930

HOW TO PASS STANDARD GRADE HISTORY

ES

A 1   You must evaluate *Source B* – that means judge its importance – as a source of information and evidence about the success of the women's suffrage movement. You should include and explain the following points:

Source B is a primary source relevant to the issue.

It presents an opinion about the success of the women's campaign.

It mentions the publicity gained by Suffragette tactics.

It contains examples of some of the methods used by the Suffragettes.

It has a reference to the death of Emily Davidson.

It comments on the unpopularity of the government.

It expresses an opinion that political change was inevitable.

However, it is written by a Suffragette supporter ('We have had the attention ...') and alleges the suffragette campaign has been successful without proof.

It makes no mention of other campaigns by womens' groups.

A 2   First of all you should use evidence from the sources which support the issue.

You should mention from *Source A*:

'The formation of the National Union of Women's Suffrage Societies in 1897 was a major step forward for the cause of women's rights' and the campaign increased 'the pressure on the government for change.'

Source B claims to have got the attention of the press and that their action has made the government unpopular. It states, 'It is only a matter of time before Mr Asquith will give way to our demands'.

Source C contains no evidence which supports the issue.

You should then identify the evidence in the sources which does not support the issue.

In *Source A* there is no appropriate evidence.

Source B suggests that even some Suffragettes did not 'understand why Emily felt it necessary to take such drastic action.'

Questions and Answers continued

Source C claims that the 'Suffragette movement, under the leadership of Mrs Pankhurst, has done much to alienate members of the government'.

The source then states that the government did not want 'to be seen to be bullied into making concessions'. The Suffragettes are describes as 'a group of extremists'.

A 3   In this answer you must reach a conclusion and decide whether or not you agree that women gained the vote because of the campaigns of the women's suffrage movement.

You should make use of source evidence used in previous answers to present a balanced summary of the arguments. You must then use your own knowledge to develop your answer further, such as women gaining the vote in other countries helped to persuade the government, the war work done by women gained them respect from the government, changes in the status of women made it almost inevitable women would get the vote eventually.

The change in prime minister – Asquith, who was against women's votes, resigned and Lloyd George, a supporter, took over.

Women over 30 gained the vote in 1918.

Railways

Technological change and its effect

What You Should Know

Until the early 19th century the main ways of travelling were by road or canal. Journeys were slow, difficult and often risky. There was a need for an efficient transport system that could carry things safely, quickly, cheaply and in bulk.

Although the usefulness of rail roads had been known for a long time railways did not become really important until the 1820s. The reason has to do with technology and new inventions. By 1830 iron rails had been invented along with the steam locomotive.

A locomotive is a steam engine that can move itself on wheels and therefore pull wagons.

You should be able to explain why a more efficient transport system was needed as Britain became more industrialised.

What you should know continued ➤

What You Should Know *continued*

Most of Britain's main railway lines were built by 1860. Railways were built by navvies who often came from Ireland or the Highlands of Scotland and their work was extremely dangerous. Navvies had a bad name for drinking and fighting and some were violent and rude – but without them railways would not have been built.

You should be able to describe in detail the difficulties and dangers of building railways. You should also be able to explain fully why some people were against building or using railways.

Railways certainly did have **economic** effects on Britain. Railways also had many **social** effects on Britain. Economic change means how business and the economy was affected. Social effects means how the lives of people were affected.

You must be able to describe the economic and social effects of railways.

Railways were at their peak in 1900 but after the First World War railways began a slow decline. Roads improved; heavy lorries could carry industrial goods and private cars took people door to door. Railways became less popular.

You should be able to describe how railways used technology to make themselves more popular with the public and also explain why railways became less important by 1930.

Questions *and* Answers

Railways – General

This source describes some railway improvements made between 1850 and 1914:

'By the late 19th century main line express trains increased their speeds to 60 mph.

In 1895 there was serious competition between the two railway companies on the London to Aberdeen route. The fastest did the 524 mile journey in eight and a half hours. Improved locomotives made these new speeds possible. Heating was gradually introduced into passenger trains.'

Questions *and* **Answers** *continued* **?**

KU Q Describe in what ways travelling by train improved between 1850 and 1930. *(4 marks)*

`KU`

From the source you should mention:

Trains became faster.

Competition between rail companies gave travellers a choice.

New locomotives were more efficient and faster.

Heating in trains made journeys more comfortable.

From your own knowledge you could mention that:

Buffet cars provided meals on trains.

Safety improved.

Toilets on board made journeys more comfortable.

Stations grew in size with small shops providing services while travelling.

ES Q The issue for investigating is:

Railways in the nineteenth century were helpful to the expansion of business.

In *Source A*, a mine owner describes the benefits of railways to his business in 1838:

'The railway has made a big difference to our operations. The coal from our mine is now distributed over a much wider area. We are also able to use the railways to bring in our supplies of timber for the galleries more cheaply as well as our own heavy machinery.'

Source B is taken from the speech of a member of Parliament in 1855:

'Since the introduction of the railways, I have seen many of the tradesmen in our villages look for other forms of employment. People no longer wish to travel by coach as the railways are faster and more comfortable. Factory owners would rather send their goods by rail than on a slow canal journey. The combined effect is to destroy men's jobs.'

Q 1 How useful is *Source A* for investigating the advantages of the introduction of railways to businesses in the nineteenth century? *(3 marks)*

Q 2   What evidence is there in *Source A* to suggest that railways in the nineteenth century were helpful to the expansion of business?

What evidence is there in *Source B* to suggest that railways in the nineteenth century were not helpful to the expansion of business? *(5 marks)*

Q 3   How far do you agree that railways in the nineteenth century were helpful to the expansion of business? Use evidence from the sources and your own knowledge to come to a conclusion.   *(4 marks)*

ES

A 1   You should use evidence from the source such as:

It is a primary source giving relevant information.

It is an opinion from a businessman affected by rail expansion.

It provides several reasons in detail about how railways assisted his business.

A 2   First of all you should use evidence from the sources which support the issue:

You should mention from *Source A*:

Heavy machinery could be brought by rail.

Supplies of timber (used as pit props) are brought to the mine by railways.

Coal could be distributed more widely.

From *Source B*:

Factory owners would rather send their goods by rail.

Railways are faster and more comfortable.

You must also remember to deal with the other part of the question.

You must select evidence which does not support the issue.

There is no evidence in *Source A* against the issue but in *Source B*:

Unemployment increased in some businesses.

People no longer wished to travel by coach.

Canal companies suffered since 'Factory owners would rather send their goods by rail than on a slow canal journey.'

Questions and Answers continued

A 3 **In this answer you *must reach a conclusion* and decide *whether or not you agree*** with the issue that railways in the nineteenth century were helpful to the expansion of business.

You should make use of source evidence used in previous answers to present a balanced summary of the arguments. You must then use your own knowledge to develop your answer further such as:

The first rail lines provided transport links in industrial areas (Glasgow–Garnkirk, for example.)

Railways boosted holiday and tourism businesses.

Industries connected to railway building boomed such as iron and steel, glass and bricks (for stations).

Farms and fishing ports benefited since perishable food could be sent to market more quickly.

Chapter 3

UNIT 1 CONTEXT C: CHANGING SCOTLAND AND BRITAIN 1880–1980

Population Change

What You Should Know

Between 1880 and 1980 the population of Britain increased from 37 million to 55 million.

The main reason for population increase was the decline in the death rate. People also lived longer. The average person could expect to live until they were 43 in 1880. By 1980 life expectancy was 78.

The distribution of population also changed. The population of Britain became urbanised. That means fewer people lived in the countryside and more lived in towns and cities. In 1881 about 35% of the population worked in farming but by 1981 only 2% did so.

You must be able to explain in detail why the population increased in size. Think widely to include changes in housing and health.

People continued to leave the Highlands of Scotland and moved to the industrial towns of central Scotland or England. Others chose to leave Britain and start a new life abroad, often in Canada, Australia or New Zealand.

You must be able to describe examples of push and pull reasons. A push reason means they were forced to go and pull reasons means people wanted to move for attractive reasons.

Make sure you understand the difference between EMIGRATION and IMMIGRATION.

What You Should Know

Irish migration continued throughout the 19th and 20th century. Irish labourers were vital in helping to build Britain's railways and in many other industries.

People from other lands also emigrated to Scotland usually to find better opportunities or escape persecution in their home lands. In the first half of the 20th century these migrants included many Italians as well as Jews escaping from Nazi Germany and Eastern Europe but after 1945 many immigrants to Scotland came from India or Pakistan.

Be able to give detailed descriptions of what groups of people chose to come to Scotland and explain why they did so.

Questions *and* Answers

Population Change – Credit

Since 1880 there have been changes in the distribution of population in Britain.

KU Q Explain the changes in the distribution of population in Britain since 1880.

KU

You should mention:

The growth of cities and the decline of rural areas. (Highland depopulation continued.)

Continuing migration from Scotland to England and parts of the Empire/ Commonwealth such as Canada, New Zealand.

Migrants to Scotland included Lithuanians, Jews and Italians before World War Two but since then many migrants have come from India, Pakistan and the West Indies. Migration to Scotland from Ireland has continued but by 1980 was declining.

UNIT 1 CONTEXT C: CHANGING SCOTLAND AND BRITAIN 1880–1980

HOW TO PASS STANDARD GRADE HISTORY

ES Q   The issue for investigating is:

Industrial change resulted in the growth of Scottish cities in the early twentieth century.

Source A is adapted from *Changing Scotland* published in 1985:

In the course of the nineteenth century, the demands of the growing industries meant that large numbers of people drifted into the cities from the neighbouring countryside where they could no longer find employment. By 1900, nearly 75% of the population of Britain was living in towns and cities.

In the early stages of this process, families had to share rooms as they wanted to stay close to their workplace, but as it continued, so the towns spread to engulf the neighbouring villages which became suburbs of the sprawling cities.

Source B is an extract from *Memories of My Father*, published in 1938.

'My father came from a mining family. He was the second oldest of a family of 12 children. He worked in the pit but then two of his cousins were killed in an accident. He decided that there was no future for him in the mining industry so he decided to leave and went to Glasgow – to join the police. His mother wouldn't speak to him when he did that. She was even more angry when his younger brother followed him.'

Source C is taken from the diary of a Glasgow minister, written in 1921:

'Since the middle of the nineteenth century, there has been a steady stream of people from Ireland to this parish. It started with the potato famine, but even after that first rush of people who fled from starvation in Ireland, there continued to be a steady stream of immigrants to Scotland who came to get away from the poverty of their homeland.'

Q 1   How useful is *Source A* as evidence of industrial change leading to overcrowding in Scottish cities in the early twentieth century?
(4 marks)

Q 2   What evidence in the sources supports the view that industrial change resulted in overcrowding in Scottish cities in the early twentieth century?

What evidence in the sources contradicts the view that industrial change resulted in overcrowding in Scottish cities in the early twentieth century?   *(6 marks)*

Questions and Answers continued

Q 3   To what extent was industrial change the cause of overcrowding in Scottish cities in the early twentieth century? Use evidence from the sources and your own knowledge to reach a balanced conclusion.
(5 marks)

ES

A 1   You must evaluate *Source A* – that means judge its importance – as a source of information and evidence about industrial change resulting in the growth of Scottish cities in the early twentieth century. You should include and explain the following points:

Source A is a secondary source giving objective factual information on the issue.

It states that large numbers of people drifted into the cities and it provides detail of the population distribution in 1900.

Towns are described as engulfing neighbouring villages therefore suggesting growth.

It states that suburbs grew around cities, a feature of urban growth.

Figure 3.1 Population change

Questions *and* Answers *continued*

A 2 Remember there are two parts to this question:

You must select and organise evidence in the sources which **do** and **do not** support the issue that industrial change resulted in the growth of Scottish cities.

In support of the issue you could mention:

From Source A:

The demands of the growing industries meant families wanted to stay close to their workplace.

From Source B:

He didn't think there was a future in the coal mine.

There is no supporting evidence in Source C.

Against the issue you could mention:

From Source A:

There is no evidence against the issue.

From Source B:

For some people it was the attraction of a new life and an escape from traditional habits and customs rather than industrial change.

From Source C:

People moved to escape starvation.

People continued to travel to urban centres to escape poverty in Ireland.

A 3   In this answer you must provide a balanced conclusion. You should make use of source evidence used in previous answers to present a balanced summary of the arguments. You must then use your own knowledge to develop your answer further such as:

The availability of jobs in cities, relative lack of jobs in countryside.

Foreign migrants settled in urban centres for many different reasons e.g. political asylum.

Cities were attractive places for country people – entertainment, excitement, opportunity to meet new people/marriage partners.

Cities offered pull reasons to move, not just negative push reasons for moving.

Health and Housing

What You Should Know

In Scottish towns in 1880 most working class people lived in tenement buildings. Often these tenements were unhealthy slums. Tenements were built quickly and cheaply. The rooms were damp with poor ventilation and light. Rents were high and few tenements had toilets, water supply or sewers. Overcrowding was a serious problem.

You must be able to describe conditions in a town slum in the mid-19th century.

You must also be able to explain why conditions in the towns were so bad.

In the countryside things were little better. Rural cottages, or black houses in the highlands, usually had rough, low stone walls, earth floors with turf or thatched roofs. These had no water supply or sanitation. Animals were often in the same room as people. To make matters worse most farm workers lived in tied houses which meant the house came with the job. A family who became unemployed also lost its home.

Watch out! If a question asks about housing conditions in Scotland you must be able to describe housing conditions in the towns AND the countryside and refer to both the Highlands and Lowlands.

What You Should Know

By the end of the 19th century it was clear that slums would have to be knocked down and new, better houses built. After the First World War (1914-1918) the government promised to build many new houses.

You should know about the housing acts which led to more council houses being built such as the Addison Act, the Wheatley Act and the Greenwood Act.

You should be able to explain how the new council estates were better than the old slums.

You should also be able to explain why some people did not like living in the new housing estates.

What you should know continued ➤

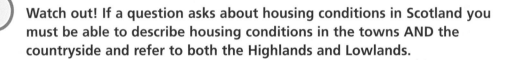

UNIT 1 CONTEXT C: CHANGING SCOTLAND AND BRITAIN 1880–1980

What You Should Know continued

After the Second World War the health and housing of working class people improved a lot.

A Welfare State was created to look after people 'from the cradle to the grave' and that included a National Health service which provided free medical care.

In the 1950s many slums were demolished and council housing estates were built. In the 1960s tower blocks were built but these new housing plans also had problems.

You should be able to describe what is meant by the welfare state and explain how the welfare state improved the lives of many people.

By 1980 health and housing for most people was better than it had been in 1880.

You should be able to describe the main differences in town life between 1880 and 1980.

Questions and Answers

Health and Housing – General

> This source describes improvements to water supplies in towns.

It was far better to stop diseases spreading by tackling their causes such as dirty water contaminated (polluted) by sewage. Water was cleaned up and by 1900 most towns had a clean supply. Proper sewage systems were built. Pipes and tunnels were laid to take waste to places where it was treated.

KU Q Describe ways in which health was improved in cities around 1900.

> **KU**
>
> From the source you should note the following:
>
> By 1900 most towns had a clean water supply.
>
> Proper sewage systems were built.
>
> Pipes and tunnels were laid to take away waste.
>
> From your own knowledge:
>
> Slum clearance was happening.
>
> Street cleaning was increasingly common in towns.
>
> Rubbish removal was also common in towns.
>
> Better quality food was available.

Questions and Answers *continued*

ES Q The issue for investigating is:

Housing improved in the first half of the twentieth century in Scotland.

Source A is from a government investigation report into Scottish housing. It was published in 1925:

'In mining villages there are still disgusting piles of human waste lying in the street. On farms, cottages are damp and badly built. In the cities there is terrible overcrowding. In the slum areas of our cities the houses are dark, unventilated and damp. However, slum clearance is helping and, in the suburbs of cities, new council houses are being built with gardens, indoor toilets and electricity.'

Source B is adapted from a school textbook:

'Most of the houses built in the 1950s were council houses. Slum clearance schemes meant that people were moved to the outskirts of the older towns or to new towns. More than five million houses were built after 1945 but in 1950 over one million homes still had no inside lavatory and 800,000 had no bath.'

Q 1 How useful is *Source A* as a source of information about housing conditions in early 20th century Scotland? *(3 marks)*

Q 2 What evidence is there in *Source A* that housing was improving in the first half of the 20th century in Scotland?

What evidence is there in *Source B* that housing was not improving in the first half of the 20th century in Scotland? *(5 marks)*

Q 3 How far did housing improve in the first half of the twentieth century in Scotland? Use evidence from the sources and your own knowledge to come to a conclusion. *(4 marks)*

ES

A 1 You must evaluate *Source A* – that means judge its importance – as a source of information and evidence that housing improved in the first half of the twentieth century in Scotland.

You should include and explain the following points, using your own knowledge where appropriate:

◆ It is a primary source from 1925 and relevant to the topic of Scottish housing.

◆ It is an official government investigation report therefore its observations are likely to be appropriate and informed.

Questions *and* Answers *continued*

- It refers to housing in several areas, not just cities.
- It refers to specific problems e.g. lack of light, ventilation, overcrowding.
- It refers to changes taking place such as slum clearance and council housing.

A 2   Remember there are *two parts* to this question.

You must *select* and *organise evidence* in the sources which **does** and **does not** support the issue that housing was improving in the first half of the 20th century in Scotland.

In support of the issue you could mention:

From Source A

Slum clearance is helping.

New council houses are being built.

The new council houses have gardens, indoor toilets and electricity.

Against the issue you could mention from *Source B*:

In 1950 over one million homes still had no inside lavatory.

In 1950 800,000 houses had no bath or shower.

A 3   In this answer you must provide a balanced conclusion. You should make use of source evidence used in previous answers to present a balanced summary of the arguments. You must then use your own knowledge to develop your answer further, such as:

- The New Towns Act planned towns such as East Kilbride and Glenrothes.
- A consequence of bombing in the Second World War was that new houses were needed quickly and 'prefabs' were a popular development after the War.
- The growth of the private owner-occupier houses improved housing in the 1930s.
- Housing legislation in the 1920s encouraged local authority building.
- Slum clearance.

Road Transport and the Car Industry

What You Should Know

During the 20th century road transport replaced railways as the most popular means of travel.

At first cars were expensive and unreliable and, for most people in towns, electric trams and buses were the common means of transport.

Lorries also began to replace horses and carts but often these operated as delivery vehicles carrying goods to and from railway stations. As road traffic increased in the 1930s road safety measures became more important.

Be able to describe some typical experiences of motorists in the late 19th and early 20th century.

Explain why road transport became more popular than using railways.

You should also be able to describe what road safety measures were introduced to make driving safer.

Be able to explain why car ownership increased.

What You Should Know

From the 1950s the increase in private car ownership and the use of road transport meant railways became less and less important. Cars became cheaper and more reliable and as a result became more popular. In 1945 there were 1.5 million cars in Britain and by 1980 this had risen to 20 million. New technology improved the reliability and safety of cars.

For most people owning a car meant they were free to go where and when they wanted. Car owners demanded more and better roads including bypasses, motorways and parking places. On the other hand, the increase in car ownership has led to concerns over safety and pollution from town planners and environmentalists.

Design two columns listing the advantages and disadvantages of increased car ownership.

HOW TO PASS STANDARD GRADE HISTORY

What You Should Know

By the 1960s the car industry employed thousands of people but by the 1980s the car industry had a reputation for bad industrial relations and poor quality cars.

Although car ownership continues to grow, you should be able to explain why the British car industry declined and almost died by the 1980s.

Questions and Answers

Road Transport – Credit

> While car ownership grew steadily between 1940 and 1980, the increase in the number of cars also created problems.

KU Q Describe fully the arguments both for and against the increase in car ownership between 1940 and 1980. *(8 marks)*

> ### KU
>
> This is an 8 mark question for which you need to write a short essay with an introduction, development of your ideas and then a conclusion.
>
> You could mention: more accidents, more pollution, more congestion, need for more roads, car parks etc. Public transport declined in importance.
>
> Greater freedom to travel, independent choice, jobs for garages, road builders. Growth of commuter suburbia.

ES Q The issue for investigating is:

> Bad industrial relations were the main problem faced by the British motor vehicle industry in the 1970s.
>
> *Source A* is from an interview with a car factory worker in 1970:

'I worked on the assembly line. It produced lots of cars but the bosses did not care how bored we were. You had so much time to do a job. If you worked quickly you could earn more money but then the bosses tried to bring in new robots to do our job so the bosses could sack us. They said the machines were needed to keep us competitive but we had to fight for our jobs. The only way to make the bosses listen was to strike. We stopped these machines.'

> *Source B* is is adapted from a book called *The Motor Car*. It was written in 1977:

Questions *and* Answers *continued*

By the end of the 1960s the British car industry had a bad name for high prices, poor quality work and late delivery.

As a result of these problems more and more people bought foreign cars. Foreign car companies used new mass production methods. Quality was good, output was high and there were almost no strikes in foreign car factories. For British car makers the result was collapse of their industry, closure of factories and redundancies.

> *Source C* is from a government report called 'Problems facing the motor vehicle industry.' It was published in 1974.

'There is not the slightest chance of the British car industry becoming competitive if the present interruptions to production caused by strikes continue. As long as British car companies fail to change to new methods of production, fail to spend money on new machinery and continue to accept below standard work then there is no hope for us. These problems are a result of the attitudes of management and the work force. Both sides are to blame for the disaster that is the British car industry.'

Q 1   To what extent do you agree that *Source A* is useful for investigating problems facing the motor vehicle industry?

Q 2   What evidence from the sources would you use to support the claim that bad industrial relations were the cause of problems facing the motor vehicle industry?

What evidence from the sources would you use to counter the claim that bad industrial relations were the cause of problems facing the motor vehicle industry?

Q 3   Were bad industrial relations the main problem facing the British motor vehicle industry? You must use evidence from the sources and recall to reach a balanced conclusion.

ES

A 1   You must evaluate *Source A* – that means judge its importance – as a source of information and evidence of the problems facing the British motor vehicle industry in the 1970s. You should include and explain the following points, using your own knowledge where appropriate.

Questions *and* **Answers** *continued*

From the source:

◆ It is a *primary source* relevant to the study period. The 1970s were a time of problems for the industry.

◆ It is an *eye witness comment* from someone who worked in a car factory.

◆ The source *illustrates the dislike* between the workers on the 'shop floor' and the managers with comments such as 'The bosses didn't care' ; new technology introduced solely 'so the bosses could sack us' but it is useful as an opinion at the time.

◆ It makes *no reference to other problems* facing the car industry.

◆ *Overall, the source is of value* since it gives some information about the problems facing the British motor vehicle industry in the 1970s.

A 2   Remember there are two parts to this question:

You must select and organise evidence in the sources which **does** and **does not** support the issue that bad industrial relations were a feature of the motor vehicle industry in the 1970s.

In support of the issue you could mention:

From Source A

'The only way to make the bosses listen was to strike.'

'the bosses didn't care how bored we were' – an indication of bad relations.

'robots were brought in to do our job so the bosses could sack us' – an indication of a lack of understanding of management actions therefore poor industrial relations between workers and bosses.

'We had to fight for our jobs.' – failure of industrial relations is conflict.

From Source B

'there were almost no strikes in foreign car factories' – by implication strikes in British company factories were damaging the industry.

From Source C

'accept below standard work' – a comment directed at poor workmanship and poor quality control indicative of poor industrial relations.

'if the present interruptions to production caused by strikes continue' – a recognition that strikes were causing big problems.

'a result of the attitudes of management and the work force' and 'Both sides are to blame for the disaster' – bad relations!

Questions and **Answers** continued

Against the issue you could mention:

From Source A

'the machines were needed to keep us competitive' – a hint that Britain was falling behind its competitors concerning new technology introduction.

From Source B

'high prices, poor quality work and late delivery' – these are problems which are not necessarily a consequence of bad industrial relations.

'more and more people bought foreign cars' – foreign competition also supported by 'Quality was good, output was high.'

'Foreign car companies used new mass production methods' – new technology was adopted by foreign companies more rapidly than UK.

'For British car makers the result was collapse of their industry, closure of factories and redundancies' – decline of industry attributed to foreign competition.

From Source C

'As long as British car companies fail to change to new methods of production.'

'fail to spend money on new machinery.'

A 3   In this answer you must provide a balanced conclusion. You should make use of source evidence used in previous answers to present a balanced summary of the arguments. You must then use your own knowledge to develop your answer further such as bad industrial relations were a problem for the industry but these problems were made worse by other reasons such as foreign competition, the attractiveness of new foreign models and the comparative slowness of introduction of new UK models and variable UK exchange rates making foreign cars cheaper.

Trade Unions and Working Conditions

What You Should Know

Trade Unions were created to put pressure on employers to improve the wages and working conditions of members. Between 1880 and 1900 trade union membership increased from half a million to over two million. Unions continued to grow in size as workers, especially unskilled workers in low pay occupations, realised the benefits of being organised in a union.

Strikes were used to force employers to improve wages and conditions.

The two most famous strikes of unskilled workers were the London Dock Strike and the Match Girls Strike. You should be able to describe what happened in those strikes and also explain why they were important to the union movement.

During the 1920s and 1930s unemployment increased and union membership fell. This was partly due to the hard times that many workers experienced as their wages fell but also because of the failure of the General Strike of 1926.

You should be able to explain the causes and results of the General Strike. You should also be able to describe the main events of the strike.

What You Should Know

After the Second World War union membership increased from 9 million in 1945 to 12 million in 1979. As unions became more national, e.g. the National Union of Miners, it was obvious that any strike could hurt the whole of the country at the same time. As a result some people argued that unions were becoming too powerful and could 'hold the country to ransom' if their demands were not met.

You should be able to describe how the NUM tried to get the Government of PM Heath to change its policies in the 1970s.

By 1980 the days of union power were ending. The new Prime Minister, Margaret Thatcher, was determined to break the power of trade unions.

Remember

This unit also covers working conditions in the home.

Think of all the kinds of 'housework' that would have to be done, usually by a woman, in 1900. One example would be clothes washing. It would be done by hand and took a very long time. Now think of how these jobs are done today, for example, by washing machines. New technology has developed many labour saving devices which has eased the lives of many women at home.

In the work place working conditions for women also improved with the Equal Pay Act and the Sex Discrimination Act, both from the 1970s.

Questions *and* Answers

Trade unions and working conditions – General

This source is from a letter to the *Edinburgh Post*, March, 1979:

'During this winter rubbish hasn't been collected and schools have been closed and all because local council workers want a wage rise. Only a few years ago in 1972 we had to suffer a three day working week and whole cities were blacked out by power cuts. All because the coal miners went on strike and electricity power stations ran out of fuel.'

KU Q Explain why public opinion turned against trade unions in the 1970s.

KU

You should include the following:

During the winter of 1978–79 rubbish was not collected and schools were closed.

The non-union public saw this was the result of local council workers wanting a wage rise.

In 1972 there was a three day working week.

Cities were blacked out by power cuts.

Coal miners were blamed for going on strike.

From recall:

During the local authority workers strike – called the 'winter of discontent' – in 1978/79 many services were stopped, even burial of dead bodies.

Prime Minister Heath raised the question of 'Who runs the country'?

Questions *and* Answers *continued*

Unions blamed for 'holding the country to ransom'.

Great personal inconvenience caused by strikes.

ES Q **The issue for investigating is:** Trades Unions improved conditions for working people in the 1970s.

Source A is a poster used in 1978 to encourage workers to join a trades union:

> **Unity is strength.**
>
> **Improve your wages and working conditions!**
>
> **How?**
>
> **Let a trade union fight for you!**
>
> You are treated badly by bosses who keep their profits high by paying you low wages.
>
> You work in dirty and dangerous conditions.
>
> You have no job security and no pension rights.
>
> In recent years union action has won better wages for miners, power workers and even local authority workers.
>
> **All workers must unite. Join a trades union now!**
>
> **The working class must be freed from exploitation!**
>
> **Make a better country for us all!**

Source B is from letter to the *Edinburgh Post*, 1978:

What are Trades Unions for?

I'm told its to help the workers but this winter graves were not dug, rubbish wasn't collected, schools were closed and all because local council workers wanted a wage rise.

Only a few years ago in 1974 we had to suffer power cuts that blacked out whole cities. All because the coal miners went on strike.

I know the early unions had to fight to get better pay and conditions but now the big unions are just bullies. It's not democratic. Why should a few people cause so much trouble for the rest of us who have got nothing to do

HOW TO PASS STANDARD GRADE HISTORY

Questions *and* Answers *continued*

with the dispute but have to suffer because of it? I'm as much working class as any union member. The unions aren't helping me.

Q 1 How useful is *Source A* about the importance of trades unions in the 1970s? *(3 marks)*

Q 2 What evidence is there in *Source A* that trades unions improved life for working people?

What evidence is there in *Source B* that trades unions did not improve life for working people? *(5 marks)*

Q 3 How far did trades unions improve life for working people? Use evidence from the sources and your own knowledge to come to a conclusion. *(4 marks)*

ES

A 1 You must evaluate *Source A* – that means judge its importance – as a source of information and evidence about the importance of trades unions in the 1970s.

◆ You should include and explain the following points, using your own knowledge where appropriate.

◆ It is a primary source relevant to the study period.

◆ There is a strong likelihood of bias since it is a pro-union poster advertising the advantages of unions.

◆ It uses emotional language – 'freed from exploitation.'

◆ It refers to the successes of unions in gaining better conditions – for miners, power workers and ... local authority workers.'

A 2 Remember there are two parts to this question.

You must select and organise evidence in the sources which ***does*** and ***does not*** support the issue that trades unions improved the life for working people in the 1970s.

In support of the issue you could mention:

From Source A:

'Many working people now have improving wages and working conditions.' The paragraph after 'Why' makes the connection between unions, better wages and conditions clear: 'because they have a trade union to fight for them.'

Questions *and* Answers *continued*

'In recent years union action has won better wages for miners, power workers and even local authority workers' – examples of union action improving life of working class.

Those without union support have bad conditions – poster refers to 'exploitation' which will only be changed through union action.

Against the issue you could mention:

From Source B:

'we had to suffer power cuts that blacked out whole cities. All because the coal miners went on strike' – discomfort caused by union action.

'this winter graves were not dug, rubbish wasn't collected, schools were closed and all because local council workers wanted a wage rise' – discomfort caused by union action.

'Why should a few people cause so much trouble for the rest of us who have got nothing to do with the dispute'.

'I'm as much working class as any union member. The unions aren't helping me' – evidence of resentment of union power caused by union action.

A 3   In this answer you must provide a balanced conclusion. You should make use of source evidence used in previous answers to present a balanced summary of the arguments. You must then use your own knowledge to develop your answer further such as:

◆ Trade union conflict in 1970s.

◆ The Industrial Relations Act.

◆ Pay freeze and pay restraint and union reaction.

◆ The Miners strike of 1974 and fall of Conservative Government.

◆ The Three Day Week.

◆ The State of Emergency.

◆ The Winter of Discontent.

◆ The fall of the Labour Government.

◆ Mrs Thatcher's victory in 1979, partly caused by a public desire to tame the unions.

Shipbuilding

What You Should Know

Shipbuilding was a very important industry in Britain and in Scotland the heart of Scottish shipbuilding was on the River Clyde.

Before the First World War Britain built 80% of the world's new ships but in the 1920s and 1930s shipbuilding faced serious problems as foreign competition increased and, as world trade declined, the need for new ships fell. However, after the Second World War there was a brief boom in shipbuilding again but old working methods remained and when modern shipyards abroad started to compete again in the 1960s British shipbuilding once again became less important.

You must be able to describe, with examples, why shipbuilding faced problems in the 1920s and 1930s but recovered for a short time in the 1950s.

You should also be able to explain why shipbuilding faced problems in the 1960s, for example, why old working methods presented a difficulty for an industry trying to compete in the modern world.

In the 1960s and 1970s the increase in containerisation and air travel also caused problems for shipbuilding while in the shipyards poor industrial relations led to a further decline in shipbuilding.

By the 1980s nationalisation had failed to save the industry and new modern working methods had come too late. Orders for ships fell as fewer ships were needed around the world and foreign builders could do the jobs more quickly and more cheaply. Most shipyards faced the risk of closure.

Questions and Answers

Shipbuilding – Credit

By the 1960s British shipbuilding was once again facing serious problems.

KU Q Explain why British shipbuilding faced difficulties in the 1960s and 1970s.

Questions and Answers continued

KU

You should mention the following in your answer:

◆ Bad industrial relations.

◆ Decline in world trade.

◆ Foreign competition.

◆ Move towards container loaded ships.

◆ New technology in ship building.

ES Q The issue for investigating is:

Modernisation in Clyde shipyards could not stop the decline of the shipbuilding industry after 1950.

Source A is adapted from a Glasgow newspaper article published in 1961:

'In the last few years we have seen the completion of new fabrication shops at the Fairfield Company which allow for the construction of large sections of the ships under cover before final assembly in one of the new building berths. There is more space allowed in the shipyards for the movement of these large prefabricated sections which allows the ships to be built in a shorter time and should attract new orders.'

Source B is taken from *The Clydeside Years* by C. U. Swones, published in 1994:

'We gathered in Frederick Street to march in protest to Glasgow Green. There were thousands of us, workers from the UCS who wanted to keep their jobs. Every man had a skill which he was enthusiastic to use and carry on the tradition of building ships on the Clyde. We knew we could get the orders for the ships if only the government would let us stay in business. But as long as foreign shipyards build faster and more cheaply than us we can not win.'

Source C is taken from a government report published in 1972:

'Most ship owners blame the inadequate delivery record of the UK yards on poor industrial relations. They do not agree on whether labour or management is primarily responsible for these poor relationships. Some believe that labour attitudes are entrenched and that management have little chance of influencing the situation. Others believe that management has lacked ability in controlling labour and has not made sufficient effort to provide adequate working conditions.'

Questions *and* Answers *continued*

Q 1   How valuable is *Source B* as evidence of the difficulties facing shipbuilding on the Clyde?   *(4 marks)*

Q 2   What evidence in the sources supports the view that modernisation in Clyde shipyards could not stop the decline of the shipbuilding industry after 1950?

What evidence in the sources disagrees with the view that modernisation in Clyde shipyards was not enough to stop the decline of the shipbuilding industry after 1950?   *(6 marks)*

Q 3   To what extent was the modernisation in Clyde shipyards unable to stop the decline of the shipbuilding industry after 1950? Use evidence from the sources and your own knowledge to reach a balanced conclusion.   *(5 marks)*

ES

A 1   You must evaluate *Source B* – that means judge its importance – as a source of evidence of difficulties facing shipbuilding on the Clyde.

Source B is useful since it is relevant to the issue of shipbuilding on the Clyde.

It is a primary source relevant to the study period. The 1970s–80s were times of problems for the industry.

Source B is from an eye witness keen to keep his job on the Clyde and who blames the government for the difficulties. This makes the source slightly biased.

It is evidence that thousands of shipyard workers were worried about the future of the industry.

It indicates that one of the main problems facing the industry was foreign competition.

It implies that the industry was facing serious difficulties since the government was relied upon to keep the industry operating.

A 2   Remember there are two parts to this question.

You must select and organise evidence in the sources which ***does*** and ***does not*** support the issue that modernisation in Clyde shipyards could not stop the decline of the shipbuilding industry after 1950.

HOW TO PASS STANDARD GRADE HISTORY

In support of the issue you could mention:

From Source A:

There is no relevant evidence.

From Source B:

It is about a demonstration because of redundancies in UCS caused by lack of orders for new ships.

Decline was inevitable 'as long as foreign shipyards build faster and more cheaply than us'.

From Source C:

It blames the decline of shipbuilding on poor management.

It comments on the decline because of poor labour attitudes.

Against the issue you could mention:

From Source A:

It shows that modernisation did take place:

◆ 'the completion of new fabrication shops'.

◆ 'final assembly in one of the new building berths.'

◆ 'allows the ships to be built in a shorter time'.

◆ And hopes that new orders should follow.

From Source B:

It claims enthusiastic support from workers and that they were confident that new orders could be won.

From Source C:

There is no evidence here against the issue.

A 3   In this answer you must provide a balanced conclusion. You should make use of source evidence used in previous answers to present a balanced summary of the arguments. You must then use your own knowledge to develop your answer further such as extensive foreign competition, there was overcapacity in British shipbuilding overall, by the 1970s there was a reduction in demand for ships and the Clyde shipyards had only really prospered during the Second World War.

Political Change and Votes for Women

See pages 28–30 for 'What You Should Know' about this topic. Then tackle the following questions.

Questions and Answers

Women and the Right to Vote – General

This source is from a school text book:

'Mrs. Pankhurst gathered around her an effective group of women who were able to speak at meetings, organise demonstrations and generally attract attention. When at first nothing seemed to happen the WSPU began to use more attention grabbing methods. They tried to disrupt political meetings, smashed windows and set fire to the contents of street corner letter boxes.'

KU Q Describe the militant tactics used by the suffragettes to try to gain votes for women.

KU

From the source you should mention:

◆ They tried to disrupt political meetings.

◆ They smashed windows.

◆ They set fire to the contents of street corner letter boxes. (Remember the earlier information about speaking at meetings is not relevant to a question about militant methods).

From recall you could mention hunger strikes, Emily Davison at the Derby and burning property belonging to important men and also trying to physically attack politicians.

ES Q The issue for investigating is:

The First World War improved the position of women in British society.

Source A is taken from a speech made in the House of Lords in 1918:

'The presentation of this Bill is recognition of the service that women have given to this country in the course of the recent conflict with Germany. Without their contribution to the struggle, our industry would have collapsed through a lack of skilled labour. We should now give the women of this country the respect which they have earned and demonstrate that respect by giving them the right to vote.'

Questions *and* Answers *continued*

Source B is taken from an Edinburgh newspaper published in May 1919:

'Women have found that the end of the war has brought an end to their new found freedom. As the men have returned from France they have gone back to their previous occupations and women have found that their services are surplus to needs. They have no choice but to return to their tiresome domestic chores either at home or in the service of a wealthy family.'

Q 1   How useful is *Source B* for investigating the issue that the First World War improved the position of women in British society? *(3 marks)*

Q 2   What evidence is there in *Source A* to suggest that the First World War improved the position of women in British society?

What evidence is there in *Source B* to suggest that the First World War did not improve the position of women in British society? *(5 marks)*

Q 3   How far do you agree that the First World War improved the position of women in British society? Use evidence from the sources and your own knowledge to come to a conclusion.   *(4 marks)*

ES

A 1   You must evaluate *Source B* – that means judge its importance – as a source of information and evidence that the First World War improved the position of women in British society.

You should include and explain the following points, using your own knowledge where appropriate:

◆ It is a primary source from a newspaper published in May 1919 and relevant to the topic of women's right to vote.

◆ It is consistent with other evidence known that the benefit of the war was short lived for many women.

◆ It shows support for the women's cause so is slightly biased in its use of language – 'end to freedom'; 'No choice'.

◆ It is very general with no detailed examples.

Questions *and* Answers *continued*

A 2 Remember there are two parts to this question. You must select and organise evidence in the sources which **does** and **does not** support the issue that the First World War improved the position of women in British society.

In support of the issue you could mention:

From Source A:

A new law was being made to give some women the right to vote.

The new law was 'recognition of the service that women have given to this country'.

'Without their contribution to the struggle, our industry would have collapsed'.

'We should now give the women of this country the respect which they have earned', 'giving them the right to vote.'

Against the issue you could mention:

From Source B:

At the end of the war there was an 'end to new found freedom'.

Women were 'surplus to needs' and men got their old jobs back.

Women had no choice but to return to their old domestic chores etc.

A 3 In this answer you must provide a balanced conclusion. You must make use of source evidence used in previous answers to present a balanced summary of the arguments. You must then use your own knowledge to develop your answer further such as:

◆ Only women over 30 given the vote initially.

◆ Women over 21 got vote in 1928.

◆ Many women did continue in women's work jobs such as service.

◆ Women's wages remained low.

◆ Facilities provided for working women during the war such as crèches were closed at the end of war.

UNIT 2 CONTEXT B: CONFLICT AND COOPERATION 1890s–1920s

Great Power Tension

What You Should Know

Before 1914 the most powerful nations in the world were in Europe. Together the main European countries were called the Great Powers.

The leader of Germany, Kaiser Wilhelm II, wanted to make Germany the strongest of the Great Powers and the other European powers were worried when they saw the Kaiser 'rocking the boat' of European peace.

At first rivalry between the other Great Powers prevented them from uniting against Germany but by 1900 the Great Powers were taking sides. Alliances were made and the network of alliances meant that a small war could easily spread into a war involving most of the Great Powers.

Be prepared to describe how Europe came to be divided into two sets of alliances, be able to use the phrase 'two armed camps' and be able to explain how a small war could spread quickly as countries joined in to help their allies.

What You Should Know

Naval rivalry also created tension between Britain and Germany. After 1906 Britain and Germany raced to build the latest, strongest battleships, which in Britain were called Dreadnoughts.

Although France and Britain did not like each other, they both feared Germany, so in 1904 a friendly agreement between France and Britain was reached. It was called the Entente Cordiale and in 1907 Britain made friends with Russia so the Triple Entente was created.

Now the Triple Entente faced the Triple Alliance which was Germany with its allies Austria–Hungary and Italy.

> Remember – although Britain did have friendly agreements with France and Russia, Britain had no alliance, which means Britain was not officially committed to helping anyone if war broke out in Europe.

Questions *and* Answers

Great Power Tension – General

> *Source A* is part of a letter by an American politician visiting Germany. It was written in April 1914:

'In the last four years German military spending has doubled. The Army leaders demand more and more money each year. Everyone here believes that Germany will be attacked by Russia and France – and since they are building up large military forces Germany must do the same. The German Naval commanders are also demanding that more warships must be built to challenge Britain's sea power.'

KU Q Why was Europe an increasingly dangerous place in the years before 1914?

KU

You should include the following points:

From the source:

◆ Military spending is increasing.

◆ German suspicion of France and Russia.

◆ An expectation of war existed.

◆ A naval race between Germany and Britain increased tension.

From recall:

◆ Alliance network.

◆ Colonial rivalry.

◆ The Kaiser's ambitions.

◆ Europe was divided into two armed camps – Britain had a friendly agreement with France and Russia. Germany had allies – Austria–Hungary and Italy. A small war could escalate.

HOW TO PASS STANDARD GRADE HISTORY

Questions *and* Answers *continued*

ES Q How useful is *Source A* as evidence for finding out about feelings in Germany before the outbreak of war in 1914? *(4 marks)*

> **ES**
>
> You must evaluate *Source A* – that means judge its importance – as a source of evidence of the arms race in Europe before 1914. You should include and explain the following points, using your own knowledge where appropriate:
>
> ◆ The source was written by an eye witness within Germany.
>
> ◆ It is a primary source from the time in question – just before the outbreak of war.
>
> ◆ The author gives a neutral, objective point of view.
>
> ◆ It gives details of German military growth.
>
> ◆ The source indicates the tension felt in Germany.
>
> ◆ The source indicates German ambitions.
>
> ◆ It is relevant to the topic.

Sarajevo and the Balkans

What You Should Know

By 1900 the Balkans region of south east Europe was an area of tension. Both Austria–Hungary and Russia wanted to control as much of the Balkans as they could. The people in the Balkans are known as Slavs and the strongest country in the Balkans, Serbia, encouraged the Slav people to fight for their independence. They did not want to be ruled over by any of the Great Powers.

However, Austria–Hungary wanted to defeat Serbia while Russia wanted to protect Serbia.

Be prepared to explain why trouble in the Balkans could trigger off a big war between the two armed camps.

What You Should Know

Europe in 1914 was like an explosion waiting to happen. The spark that set off the explosion was caused by the murder of two people in a town called Sarajevo.

By 1914 Serbia had become stronger and Austria–Hungary was looking for any excuse to destroy Serbia. Tension between Austria–Hungary and Serbia had been high since 1908 when the Austrians had taken over a Balkan country called Bosnia. Serbia and Russia wanted to get revenge against Austria–Hungary. The chance for action came in June 1914.

On June 28th 1914, the Archduke Franz-Ferdinand, heir to the Austrian throne, visited Sarajevo, the capital of Bosnia. Security was poor and the archduke and his wife were assassinated by a terrorist gang called the Black Hand Gang. The assassinations in Sarajevo was the excuse that Austria–Hungary needed.

 Be able to describe the events in Sarajevo on June 28th 1914.

What You Should Know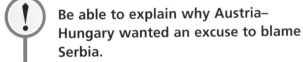

Austria–Hungary blamed Serbia for the assassination and sent an ultimatum to Serbia.

An ultimatum means an order to do something, or else. Austria–Hungary was encouraged by Germany to provoke Serbia into fighting so did not want Serbia to accept the ultimatum. When Serbia refused to accept all points in the ultimatum Austria–Hungary declared war on Serbia.

Be able to explain why Austria–Hungary wanted an excuse to blame Serbia.

What You Should Know

When Austria declared war on Serbia the network of alliances started to drag the Great Powers into a war. At the last minute most European leaders realised they did not really want a war – but it was too late.

Germany had promised to help Austria–Hungary but that would mean fighting against France and Russia at the same time. To solve the problem of a two front war, Germany had created the Schlieffen Plan to win the war against France and Russia. The plan's success depended on a surprise attack on France through Belgium but Britain had made a promise to protect Belgium if it was attacked or invaded.

When Germany invaded Belgium as part of the Schlieffen Plan, Britain declared war on Germany on August 4th 1914.

You must be able to describe accurately the sequence of events which show the Great Powers being dragged into war. You must also be able to use the word mobilisation in your description.

Questions *and* Answers

Balkan tensions and assassination at Sarajevo – Credit

> The next major war, Bismarck predicted, would be sparked off by 'some damned foolish thing in the Balkans' (Bismarck was a 19th century German politician).

KU Q Assess the importance of the assassinations at Sarajevo in 1914 in starting a war in Europe.

KU

The information you include in this answer and the time spent on it depend on whether it is an 8 mark or 4 mark question.

You must include the following points:

◆ You should outline briefly the tensions in the Balkans before the assassination, especially those between Austria–Hungary, Serbia and Russia.

◆ The assassination gave Austria–Hungary the opportunity to provoke Serbia into a war.

Questions *and* **Answers** *continued* ?

◆ The conflict with Serbia brought Russia into a war with Austria–Hungary but by that time, late July 1914, the alliance system had been triggered and France and Germany also entered the conflict. As part of Germany's plan to fight Russia and France simultaneously, the Schlieffen Plan required Germany to attack France by way of Belgium and that led to Britain entering the war.

◆ You could also mention that these consequences of the assassination were waiting to happen and the assassination was just a convenient spark.

ES Q *Source A* was written by the Austrian Chancellor, Count Berchtold, in 1909:

When we eventually attack Serbia we must try to ensure that it will not be seen in Russia as an act of aggression. I believe we can arrange this by attacking Serbia only when their actions become openly hostile.

Source B is by one of the judges at the trial of Gavrilo Princip in 1914:

I believed that Austria was looking for an excuse for war with Serbia. They may have deliberately sent the Archduke Franz-Ferdinand to Sarajevo in the hope that this would provoke an incident.

To what extent are the opinions of the author of *Source B* supported by the evidence in *Source A*? *(6 marks)*

ES

◆ Both agree that Austria wanted war and that Serbia should be made to look the guilty party in causing the conflict.

◆ *Source B* suggests that Franz Ferdinand was deliberately sent to Sarajevo in the hope a crisis would erupt. By blaming the assassination on Serbia that matches with *Source A* saying that Serbia must be made to look hostile.

◆ *Source B*'s belief that Austria wanted an excuse is supported by the Austrian Chancellor, in *Source A*, writing that 'we can arrange this' – meaning an excuse to attack Serbia but not provoke Russia.

The outbreak of war

What You Should Know

When war broke out in August 1914, every one thought that it would be over by Christmas. All over Europe people were excited about a war they thought would be short and victorious. Britain only had a small army compared to the other Great Powers and needed volunteers. A propaganda campaign was started to persuade young men to join the army.

In the first few weeks of the war nearly half a million British men joined the army. The government's recruitment campaign was a big success.

Remember

You should be able to describe the ways the government persuaded young men to join the armed forces.

You should also be able to explain why people were excited and enthusiastic about the war at first but how that attitude changed as the war went on.

Questions *and* Answers

Recruitment and the outbreak of war – General

Source A is from a recent book about the First World War:

'When German troops marched into Belgium the newspapers were full of stories of Germans killing, burning and raping their way across 'Brave Little Belgium'. Posters persuaded young men that their king and country needed, or that their wives and girlfriends expected, them to go and fight. Within a few weeks the army had more volunteers than they could cope with.'

KU Q Explain why so many young men volunteered for the British army in August 1914.

KU

From the source:

◆ Germany had invaded Belgium.

Questions *and* Answers *continued*

- Newspaper stories reported German atrocities in Belgium.
- Poster campaigns used patriotism to persuade people to join up.
- Posters also made men felt they were letting down their wives and girlfriends if they did not join up.

From your own knowledge:

- Britain had a promise to protect Belgium from attack.
- Propaganda campaigns were effective.
- Germans were shown as monsters on posters.
- Men joined up for excitement and adventure.
- Men did not want to miss the adventure since it was expected to be over by Christmas.

ES Q *Source B* is taken from the diary written by Andrew Ramage:

13 September 1914

'We left the barracks in Aberdeen at 9.20 p.m. singing a few army songs. A pipe band and a brass band played in front of us. We hope to get to the see some fighting before it is all over. I'd like to win some medals. Crowds lined the streets and cheered. Sweethearts galore broke their hearts and I got a small collection of presents, mostly cigarettes from absolutely unknown females.'

How useful is *Source B* as evidence of the attitudes of people to the Great War in 1914?

ES

You should mention:

- It is an eyewitness account from the time.
- It is relevant to the topic since it is a diary of a soldier leaving for the war in 1914.
- It shows the hopes of a soldier going to war – 'We hope to get to see some fighting before it is all over. I'd like to win some medals.'
- It shows the reaction of the public – people cheered and lined the streets.
- Soldiers were given presents as they left.

Deadlock and Trench Warfare

What You Should Know

When the Schlieffen Plan failed both sides dug lines of trenches to protect the ground they were defending. By the end of 1914 all hopes for a quick war had gone and the two sides occupied lines of trenches stretching from the Belgian coast to the Swiss border. This was the Western Front.

Defending was much easier than attacking. New weapons such as machine guns made it very difficult to attack an enemy that was dug in to trenches and protected by barbed wire. The war had become deadlocked which means that neither side could break through the defences of the other side. Sometimes the word stalemate is used to describe the same thing.

You should be able to explain why the Schlieffen Plan failed.

You should also be able to describe a typical trench system and explain why defence was easier than attack.

The trenches were home to British, Commonwealth, German and French soldiers. For four years these soldiers fought each other over no-man's-land. Trenches were dug to make it easier to resist an enemy attack. They provided a shelter where the soldiers ate and slept. They also provided protection from artillery and machine gun fire and were a base to attack from.

Conditions in the trenches were very bad. Disease spread, there were lice and rats, and the danger made some soldiers kill themselves.

Watch out for questions that ask about warfare on the Western Front and others which ask about trench conditions and trench life. Trench warfare and trench life questions require different sorts of information in your answers.

What You Should Know

Most battles on the western front followed a similar pattern. They usually started with a big artillery bombardment to destroy enemy defences and push enemy soldiers out of their trenches. Then the infantry went 'over the top' and advanced towards the enemy front lines. One of the most famous battles was the Battle of the Somme.

The battle started with a five day and night artillery barrage intended to destroy the German wire and any defending soldiers but when the British went over the top on the 1 July 1916, they were almost wiped out. The attack had failed but it dragged on until September.

Generals believed in the idea of attrition and high losses were accepted as part of the plan to grind down the enemy.

You should be able to describe the aims of the Battle of the Somme and then explain why these aims were not achieved.

Questions and Answers

Deadlock and Trench Warfare – Credit

KU Q   Describe briefly trench warfare on the Western Front.

KU

You should include in your answer:

Trench raids.

Artillery barrages.

Over the top infantry advance.

Features of defence that had to be overcome – no-man's-land, machine guns, barbed wire.

Specific examples could help, e.g. Battle of Somme.

Use of gas and tanks later in the war.

Huge loss of life.

Questions *and* Answers *continued*

ES Q *Source A* was written by an army officer to the Prime Minister in January 1915:

'The present war has changed all ideas about modern warfare. The problem to be solved on the Western Front is how to get across open space and barbed wire entanglements in the face of machine gun fire and concentrated artillery fire. Fields, roads and trees are torn up and twisted by explosions. Trenches are dug to protect soldiers from the artillery fire. How long must we send young men to chew barbed wire in Flanders?'

What is the attitude towards fighting on the Western Front shown in *Source A*?

ES

The attitudes towards fighting shown in the source include:

- Attack is a problem.
- A solution must be found.
- Trenches are essentially defensive and are protection – they will not win the war.
- Frontal attacks are costly in human life and will achieve little.

New Technology

What You Should Know

New technology such as gas and tanks were used to break the deadlock on the Western Front.

At first gas was an effective weapon since unprotected troops were terrified of it but better gas masks reduced its importance. Gas was also unreliable since it could blow back if the wind changed or since it was heavier than air it lay in ground hollows making it difficult for troops to advance.

Tanks had huge advantages. They could crash across no-man's-land, break barbed wire and provide cover for advancing troops but they also had disadvantages. They got stuck in soft ground, were slow and difficult to steer and were easy targets for artillery.

Neither weapon was really a breakthrough in trench warfare.

You should be able to describe the advantages and disadvantages of several examples of new weapons technology. You should also be able to explain which of the new weapons were most successful and why.

What You Should Know

Submarines were effective examples of new technology.

The Germans use submarines to attack supply ships heading for Britain. The idea was to starve Britain into surrender. By 1917 food in Britain was being rationed but Britain fought back with the convoy system.

At first aircraft were used for scouting missions but as technology developed they became combat fighters and some carried small bombs. By the end of the war large bombers were being developed to bomb German cities. During the war large airships called Zeppelins were used by Germany to bomb London but they were not very effective.

Questions and Answers

New Technology – General

> This is a scientific war – aeroplane, chlorine gas, deadly accurate artillery and tanks dominate the battlefield.

KU Q Describe briefly the use of new technology in attempting to break the deadlock on the Western Front.

KU

Mention should be made of gas, tanks and perhaps aircraft. At least two detailed points should be made about how each of these weapons were used to break the deadlock, for example, tanks provided cover for men crossing no-man's-land and tanks could burst through barbed wire.

ES Q *Source A was written on 3 May 1915:*

One of our men returned from hospital where he had seen gas-stricken men gasping for breath and dying like flies while the medical people could do nothing for them.

HOW TO PASS STANDARD GRADE HISTORY

Questions and Answers continued

Source B was written on 5 May 1915:

'A tin ... filled with filthy water from the field behind is hung up in each section of the trench along with a bag of clothes. When the poisonous fumes which the Germans pour on our trenches are seen, the sentry has to give each man a wet cloth to put over his face.'

How useful are *Sources A* and *B* as evidence of the British army's readiness to cope with a gas attack?

ES

The sources are useful in that they show the lack of readiness to cope with gas attacks in 1915. Gas was first used as a weapon in that year and since there were no gas masks prepared men had to retreat or suffer serious injury.

You should quote extracts from the sources and link them to the question, such as in *Source A* 'the medical people could do nothing for them' and in *Source B* 'the sentry has to give each man a wet cloth to put over his face,' suggesting a lack of readiness to cope.

The Home Front in Britain

What You Should Know

The whole of Britain was involved in the war effort. The Government made new laws such as the **Defence of the Realm Act (Dora)** which allowed the Government to control anything in Britain which affected the war effort, including industries such as coal mining.

The phrase 'Home Front' means that civilians back in Britain were needed to help in the war effort.

All information was **censored**, including private letters from soldiers and also newspapers.

The Government encouraged everyone to do their bit to help win the war in different ways.

The Government used propaganda posters during the war which encouraged people to hate the Germans or join the army or save food.

What you should know continued ➤

What You Should Know continued

By 1916 men aged between 18 and 41 were conscripted (ordered) into the army. Those who refused were called Conscientious Objectors (Conchies) and treated like criminals.

You should be able to explain why some men became conscientious objectors and describe what happened to them.

What You Should Know

When the war started the Suffragettes stopped their campaign for women's votes and campaigned instead for the war effort. Women took over men's jobs such as bus and train drivers, police duties and making ammunition in munition factories. At the end of the war women over 30 were given the right to vote, partly as a thank you for their war efforts.

You must be able to describe the types of work done by women during the war.

What You Should Know

By 1917 food was in short supply so the Government started to ration food. People were encouraged not to waste food and to grow vegetables in their gardens.

Overall, you should be able to describe several ways the Government tried to control or influence everyday life in Britain during the war and also explain why the Government thought it was necessary to increase their control.

Questions *and* Answers

The Home Front – General

Source A is about the introduction of conscription in 1916:

'When soldiers came home on leave they brought stories of the horrors of the trenches. Everywhere people were aware of the increasing casualty lists. Women were no longer happy to see their men going off to war. Less and less men were volunteering for the army so the government introduced conscription for all fit men aged between eighteen and forty-five years old.'

KU Q Why did the British Government introduce conscription in 1916?

KU

From the source:

♦ Soldiers on leave told how bad conditions were in the trenches were.

♦ Fewer people were willing to volunteer.

♦ Casualties were high.

♦ Women no longer keen to persuade their men to join up.

From your own knowledge:

♦ The army needed to replace the men already killed.

♦ Trench warfare and large battles were causing huge casualties.

ES Q In *Source B* a woman describes how she felt when her son was conscripted into the army in 1917.

They took my husband and Andy, my eldest boy. Now they want Tom. He is all I have left. I can't bear the thought of losing Tom but they don't seem to care that I've already lost my man and a son. They say he's got to fight for his king and country. Why can't they make peace with the Germans? If it was left to the mothers we would stop the fighting tomorrow.

Discuss the attitude to the war shown in *Source B*.

ES

♦ The woman is against the war.

♦ She does not want her son to be conscripted.

♦ Her husband and son are dead.

♦ She doesn't want her younger son to be called up and perhaps killed.

♦ She does not think it is fair that her young son is being called up – 'I've already lost my man and a son.'

♦ The woman wants an end to the war.

The End of the War and the Treaty of Versailles

What You Should Know

By 1918 Russia had surrendered and Germany could transfer all its troops to the Western Front. The Americans had entered the war against Germany at the end of 1917 but it would be some time before US troops arrived in France in large numbers. In April 1918 the Germans began a massive attack on the Western Front in a final effort to break through.

At first the German Spring offensive succeeded and advanced to within 60 km of Paris. By July they were halted and the allies pushed them back. By summer 1918 over a million US troops were now in Europe, the British naval blockade was causing serious shortages of food and war materials in Germany and Germany's allies were on the verge of collapse. By November it was clear Germany could not win the war.

You should be able to describe the problems facing Germany in 1918 and be able to explain why Germany accepted an armistice in November 1918.

What You Should Know

When the Armistice was signed on 11 November 1918 the fighting stopped and in June 1919 a peace treaty was signed with Germany which officially ended the Great War. It was called the Treaty Of Versailles. The treaty punished Germany but pleased none of the allied war leaders. Germany was blamed for starting the war (war guilt) and had to pay compensation (reparations). Germany was left bitter and wanting revenge.

You must be able to describe the terms of the Treaty of Versailles and explain why Germany felt so angry with them.

Questions and Answers

The End of the War and the Treaty of Versailles – General

Source A was written by a visitor to Germany just after the war ended:

'In the last months of the war the people in Germany were suffering. The British naval blockade stopped food and other essential supplies getting to Germany. Coal was in short supply which led to power cuts. Rationing reduced scarce food even further and people scavenged in fields and gutters for scraps of rotting food.'

KU Q Describe the difficulties faced by the German people during 1918.

KU

From the source:
- Naval blockade caused food shortages.
- Naval blockade caused shortages of essential supplies.
- Coal shortages for fuel.
- Power cuts.
- Rationing increased.
- People had to scavenge for food.

From your own knowledge:
- Health problems increased.
- A flu epidemic hit Germany badly.
- Industrial production collapsed.
- There were heavy casualties.
- Falling morale made the war seem pointless.

ES Q *Source B* is from a biography of Georges Clemenceau who represented France at the Treaty of Versailles:

'Clemenceau was a firm believer in the view that you must not negotiate with a German; you must dictate to him: on no other terms will a German respect you. Clemenceau was convinced that the negotiations at Versailles had to treat Germany firmly. He had twice seen his beloved France invaded by Germans in his lifetime. He was determined it must never happen again.'

Questions *and* Answers *continued*

How important were Clemenceau's views on how Germany should be treated after the First World War?

> **ES**
>
> ◆ His views were important as he was the representative of France, a major power and victor.
>
> ◆ He wanted no negotiation with Germany.
>
> ◆ Germany should be dictated to and that is what happened.
>
> ◆ He was determined to leave Germany weakened.
>
> ◆ He did not want France attacked again.
>
> From recall:
>
> ◆ Clemenceau was not prepared to compromise.
>
> ◆ He was one of the Big Three. His views dominated the final treaty.

 For more examples of questions about Versailles see the section on Germany 1918–1939.

The League of Nations and the Search for Security

Many people hoped the Great War had been a war to end all war, so the allies agreed to create a League of Nations to provide peace and security for all countries.

 You should be able to explain what the League of Nations was meant to achieve and describe some of the difficulties it faced. You should also be able to describe some of the main parts of the League of Nations and what their purpose was.

What You Should Know

The League of Nations tried to encourage nations to disarm. **Disarmament** is the opposite of the arms race which people believed had been a main cause of the war. The League believed that countries would feel more secure if everyone disarmed. In 1928 world powers promised they would never again go to war in an agreement called the Kellogg Pact. However, by the end of the 1920s the idea of trust, cooperation and security based on disarmament was fading fast.

Be able to explain why disagreements over disarmament broke out and why some countries were not prepared to cooperate with the ideas of the League of Nations.

Questions and Answers

The League of Nations and the Search for Security – Credit

An early difficulty faced by the League of Nations was that some nations did not want to join.

KU Q What were the main weaknesses of the League of Nations?

> **KU**
>
> *The information you include in this answer and the time spent on it depends on whether it is an 8 mark or 4 mark question.*

You must include most of the following points:

◆ It was not a League of all nations.

◆ The USA did not join and that weakened the League.

◆ Russia did not join at first.

◆ Germany did not trust the League since it was created by the victors after the Great War.

◆ Britain and France were the main powers in the League but they were weakened by the war.

◆ France often disagreed with the aims of the League, especially disarmament.

◆ France wanted revenge and remained suspicious of Germany.

◆ France did not trust the League and still relied on a system of alliances created in the 1920s for its security.

◆ The League had no army to enforce its decisions.

ES Q *Source A* was written by a newspaper reporter at the Versailles Peace Conference:

Even after all the slaughter of the Great War the leaders of Europe could not forget their old rivalries and hatreds. The result is that the world will get a League of Nations but it will have little power and it will be unable to influence nations or events. America has chosen not to become involved

Questions *and* Answers *continued*

and so the League will reflect only the interests of the victors, especially France. What chance is there of a lasting peace while revenge dominates the thinking of the victors?

> What is the attitude of the newspaper reporter towards the peace settlement and the League of Nations?

ES

The reporter feels that:

◆ Little has been gained or learned from the conflict – 'Even after all the slaughter … the leaders of Europe could not forget their old rivalries and hatreds.'

◆ A League of Nations will exist but it will be weak.

◆ Peace will not last and war will come.

◆ The League will not reflect all opinion, only those who want to use it for their own purposes.

◆ Future conflict is almost inevitable.

◆ France is identified as being unlikely to work for the aims of the League.

◆ Overall, he feels a chance has been lost to secure peace.

UNIT 2 CONTEXT C: CONFLICT AND COOPERATION 1930s–1960s

The Road to War 1935–1939

What You Should Know

Hitler promised to rebuild German pride and power and in March 1935 he announced to the world that Germany was rearming. Hitler also announced that he was increasing the size of the German army by starting conscription. Both of these actions had been banned by the Treaty of Versailles.

Britain reached an agreement called the the Anglo German Naval treaty which allowed Germany to build up its navy, including submarines.

In the spring of 1936 Hitler broke international treaties by moving soldiers into the Rhineland, an area of Germany which had been demilitarised by the Treaty of Versailles.

You should be able to describe in detail what Hitler did to rebuild Germany's power, pride and strength between 1933 and 1939. You should also be able to explain the effect of his actions on other countries and describe how they felt as they saw Germany getting stronger.

What You Should Know

After 1936 Hitler could not have been stopped without a major war. Britain and France, the other main European powers at the time, were afraid of war so tried to appease Hitler.

Appeasement meant giving in to Hitler hoping he would make no more demands. The climax of appeasement happened during the crisis over Czechoslovakia.

You should be able to describe what the Sudetenland was and explain why Hitler wanted it. Be able to explain why the agreement reached at Munich in September 1938 caused such divided opinion.

What you should know *continued* ➤

What You Should Know continued

Britain promised to protect Hitler's next likely target which was Poland. It seemed unlikely that Britain could do much to help Poland, especially when Hitler made an agreement with Stalin. This agreement was called the Nazi Soviet Non Aggression Pact and it shocked the world.

On 1 September 1939 Nazi forces attacked Poland and on 3 September 1939 Britain declared war on Germany. Appeasement had ended and war had begun.

Questions and Answers

The Road to War 1935–1939 – General

Source A is part of a speech by Adolf Hitler in March 1935:

'Sixteen years have passed since we were made to disarm. Today I say to the world that once again Germany will be strong, but only so that we can defend ourselves and also give our people jobs making the weapons we need for our defences.'

KU Q Explain why Germany began to rearm in 1935.

KU

From the source:

◆ Germany resented having to disarm.

◆ Hitler wanted Germany to be strong.

◆ Hitler claimed rearming was for defensive reasons.

◆ Rearmament would provide jobs for German people.

From your own knowledge:

◆ Hitler had ambitions for Germany to expand.

◆ Rearmament was necessary for any future war.

◆ Hitler had promised to destroy the Treaty of Versailles and disarmament was part of the treaty.

◆ Hitler wanted to take revenge on France and Britain.

HOW TO PASS STANDARD GRADE HISTORY

> ## Questions *and* Answers *continued*

ES Q   *Source B* is from a book called '*The Guilty Men*':

'The Chamberlain Government made three serious mistakes. Firstly, they failed to introduce a much-needed programme of rearmament. Secondly, they gave in to Hitler over Czechoslovakia when they did not need to do so. Thirdly, they did not make a serious effort to build an alliance with Russia in 1939. The result was that in 1939 Britain entered the war with fewer allies than she could have had in 1938.'

Are the opinions about the Chamberlain government in *Source B* justified?

ES

Your answer should say the criticisms are *partly* justified:

◆ The source says the Chamberlain Government failed to introduce rearmament. Rearmament was started in Britain but perhaps too late.

◆ The source says Chamberlain gave in to Hitler when he did not need to do so – that is partly true as Czechoslovakia had strong defences. France and Britain and Czechoslovakia together might have defeated Germany. Germany might have backed down, but all the advice given to Chamberlain by his advisers was to appease.

◆ It is true that Britain did not make a serious attempt to build an alliance with Russia since Britain disliked Communist Russia and believed there was no rush.

Figure 5.1 The Road to War 1935–1939

The experience of war 1939–45

What You Should Know

During the Second World War civilians were caught up in the war, either by fighting in their towns and cities, bombing by enemy aircraft and rockets or by being involved in war work. In most countries governments took charge of everyday life in order to ensure that the country worked together to win the war. Everyone was affected by the war.

Be ready to describe several ways the war affected people's lives. You should be able to use accurately words such as rationing, evacuation, blitz, conscription, censorship and blackouts.

Also be prepared to deal with questions about civilian experiences in both Britain and Germany.

Questions and Answers

The Experience of War 1939–45 – Credit

> During the Second World War civilians were in the front line of attack.

KU Q Describe fully civilian life during the Second World War in EITHER (a) Britain OR (b) Germany

(Note: for this answer you should write a short essay of several paragraphs.)

KU

Remember, you must choose to write about the effects of the war on civilians in either Germany OR Britain.

In this short essay you must *start with a brief introduction outlining the points you will develop in your answer*. Then you must *write several paragraphs*. Write a *new paragraph for each separate topic*. For example, you could write a paragraph on *civil defence* and precautions taken against bombing, the *effects of bombing* and *rationing*, the *Home Guard* and so on. You could also deal with the effect of the war on *morale* and *how people relaxed or entertained themselves*. You could *mention evacuation in Britain* and *for Germany the experience of having night and day bombing attacks leading to defeat of the nation*.

The following sources are about the effects of the war on German civilians.

In *Source A* a German woman living in Hamburg in 1943 describes the aftermath of a British air raid:

'The following morning all women and children had to be evacuated from the city. It was dreadful. There was no gas, no electricity, not a drop of water. It is hard to imagine the panic and the chaos. We had only one idea – to escape.'

ES Q   In *Source B* a modern historian assesses the effects of the Allied bombing of Germany:

'In Berlin the damage was severe enough to cause many to leave the city and to close all the schools but less than half of the city's industries stopped work and many of the stoppages were brief. Morale did not break in Berlin or Hamburg.'

To what extent do *Sources A* and *B* agree about the Allied bombing campaign?

ES

The sources agree on the following points:

◆ People left the city.

◆ There was damage to property or services.

◆ The sources differ in the description of damage. *A* mentions there was no gas, electricity or water supplies but *B* only mentions schools closing.

◆ The sources also disagree on some points: *A* says many services collapsed but *B* states that less than half the city's industries stopped work.

◆ *A* describes panic and the desire for escape among the people but *B* says morale did not break. Source *A* implies that morale did break.

Warfare and New Technology

In the First World War the conflict became bogged down in lines of trenches but in the Second World War new technology meant the war covered huge areas and the fighting spread around the world.

i You should be able to explain the effects of new technology, especially bombing of cities, and the use of tanks, submarines and rockets. Remember, of course, that the first ever nuclear weapon, the A-bomb, was used at the end of the Second World War against Japan. It was dropped by a plane named Enola Gay, not fired by a missile.

Questions and Answers

Warfare and New Technology – General

> *Source A* gives evidence about the atomic bomb dropped on Hiroshima, Japan, on 6 August 1945:

'There was a glaring, pinkish light in the sky which burned people's eyes out. Anyone within a kilometre of the explosion became a bundle of smoking black charcoal within seconds. Within minutes about 70,000 people were dead.'

KU Q What were the effects of the dropping of the atomic bomb on Hiroshima?

KU

From the source, the effects were:

◆ A greyish pinkish light in the sky.

◆ The eyes of people were burned out.

◆ Human beings were turned into smoking black charcoal if within one kilometre of the explosion.

◆ 70,000 people were dead.

From your own knowledge you could mention:

◆ Long term radiation illness.

◆ Shock and disbelief in the Japanese government.

◆ The Hiroshima bomb was an important factor in forcing Japan to surrender.

◆ It marked the start of the age of nuclear weapons.

ES Q *Source B* is from a US report explaining why the atomic bomb was used against Japan. It was written in 1949:

'The atomic bomb was a weapon that would end the war and save a million American lives. Remember we were dealing with a people who did not hesitate to make a sneak attack on Pearl Harbour destroying not only ships but also the lives of thousands of American sailors.'

Questions and **Answers** *continued*

Source C is by Admiral Leahy, Chief of Staff to President Truman in 1945:

'In my opinion this dreadful weapon did not help in our war against Japan. They were already defeated and were ready to give up because of the sea blockade and successful conventional bombing raids. If we had promised to let them keep their Emperor the Japanese would have quickly surrendered.'

Compare the views about the use of the atom bomb against Japan in Sources B and C.

ES

◆ B supports the use of the bomb but C calls it a dreadful weapon.

◆ B says the bomb ended the war but C says it was unnecessary.

◆ B suggests the war would have dragged on costing lives but C says the Japanese were ready to surrender.

◆ C provides reasons why the Japanese were near defeat but B does not.

◆ B seems to want to use the bomb to punish Japan but C makes no mention of that.

Britain, Superpowers and the United Nations

What You Should Know

After 1945 America and Russia became world superpowers and Britain became less important as a world power. By the 1950s Britain was closely linked to American policy for its defence.

 You must be able to describe what is meant by NATO and nuclear deterrence.

What You Should Know

During the war Britain, America and Russia all fought together against Nazism. After the war, however, Russia and America, supported by Britain, became enemies in the Cold War. Europe was split between the Communist bloc (no K!) and the 'West'. The two parts were divided by the Iron Curtain. America wanted to stop the spread of Communism while Russia wanted to do the opposite. The superpowers – Russia and America – came close to war on several occasions.

You must be able to use the phrases 'Cold War' and 'Iron Curtain' accurately and explain what they mean.

 You should be able to describe the occasions when war was close, including the Berlin Airlift, the Korean War in 1953, the building of the Berlin Wall in 1961 and the Cuban Missile Crisis in 1962.

What You Should Know

The United Nations was created at the end of the war to settle disputes peacefully, protect human rights and improve co-operation between nations. Although the UN helped keep the peace in small disputes, when it came to big arguments between the superpowers the UN had very little influence.

You should be able to describe how the UN operated, what its aims were and also some of its successes.

On the other hand, you must be able to explain how superpower rivalry limited the effectiveness of the UN.

Questions and Answers

Britain, Superpowers and the UN – General

Source A is from a book about the Cold War written in 1970:

'Europe is divided by an Iron Curtain. In the West the people are free, enjoy a good standard of living and can come and go as they please. Behind the Iron Curtain people are not free, they live poor, hungry lives and have no freedom. Where would you want to live?'

Questions and Answers continued

KU Q Describe the differences between the Communist bloc and the 'West'.

KU

From the source:

In the West the people are free but not in Communist Europe.

In the West the people have a better standard of living.

In the West the people can travel freely but not in Communist Europe.

From your own knowledge:

The Communist Party was the only political party in Eastern Europe. In the West there was more choice. Russia controlled the the countries in Eastern Europe but Russia had no influence in western Europe.

There was censorship in the East but in the West people could read and watch what they chose.

ES Q *Source B is from a speech by Stalin about Russian membership of the United Nations:*

'Even as members, we do not trust the United Nations as a peacekeeping body. As a matter of fact, the UN is not a united, world-wide organisation formed to keep peace. It is an organisation for the Americans acting for the needs of American aggression.'

What was Stalin's opinion of the United Nations?

ES

Stalin did not trust the UN.

Stalin did not believe it was a united world-wide organisation.

Stalin did not believe it was formed to keep peace.

Stalin believed the UN was an organisation set up to help America.

However, Stalin was prepared to remain in the United Nations (from your own knowledge) as it gave Russia influence (and a veto) as a permanent member of the Security Council.

The Berlin Crises

In 1949, and again in 1961, crises in Berlin almost started a Third World War:

Crisis One

In 1945 Germany was divided into four zones controlled by the USA, the USSR, Britain and France. Berlin was in the Russian zone but because it was the capital of Nazi Germany it was also split into four zones.

Stalin, the Russian leader, wanted the Western powers out of Berlin so in 1948 Stalin ordered that all land communications with Berlin should be shut down. The Western allies responded by operating the Berlin Airlift.

Key Points

You must be able to describe the division of Germany after the Second World War and also explain why it happened. You must also be able to use the following words and phrases accurately and appropriately – Cold War, the 'Western allies', blockade, airlift.

Crisis Two

Stalin still hated West Berlin being in the heart of East Germany. He wanted to stop people in the Communist controlled countries escaping into West Berlin and Stalin also wanted to stop West Berlin being used as a spy base against East Germany.

In 1961 the Russians built a wall right across Berlin and stopped people travelling between East and West Berlin. People who tried to get across the wall were killed.

Key Points

Be able to describe in detail why Stalin was annoyed by the existence of West Berlin and explain what the wall was meant to do.

You should also be able to explain how the wall represented the division of Europe between the Communist East and the 'West'.

Questions *and* Answers

The Berlin Crises – Credit

> In 1948 the Cold War nearly became a 'hot war'; the cause – Berlin.

KU Q Explain why Berlin became a crisis point in East-West relations during 1948–1949.

KU

Your answer should contain most of the following:

◆ Berlin, and Germany, were divided at end of World War Two. All of Berlin was inside the Russian zone yet America and Britain and France had access to their zones, therefore could travel over Communist controlled Eastern Germany.

◆ Stalin was worried about Western plans to unite their zones in western Germany.

◆ Stalin wanted to push USA/GB/France out of Berlin.

◆ Stalin cut off all land and water contacts between the 'West' and Berlin.

◆ The West responded by organising contact by air – the Berlin Airlift. Had Stalin stopped or attacked any aircraft flying into Berlin a major war could have started.

ES Q *Source A is from a speech by President Kennedy in West Berlin, 26 June 1963:*

'While the wall is the most obvious and vivid demonstration of the failures of the Communist system, for all the world to see, we take no satisfaction in it, for it is, as your Mayor has said, an offence not only against history but an offence against humanity, separating families, dividing husbands and wives and brothers and sisters, and dividing a people who wish to be joined together.'

> What had happened to cause President Kennedy to make this speech?

ES

You should mention most of the following points in your answer:

◆ Berlin was a source of East/West tension since 1945.

◆ East Germany stopped free travel between East and West Berlin in 1961.

◆ East Berlin then built a wall dividing the city.

◆ People were killed as they tried to escape to the West across the wall.

◆ Kennedy wanted to show his support for the people of West Berlin who felt threatened by Communist action.

◆ Kennedy wanted to show himself as a strong president against Communism.

◆ Kennedy wanted to build on his success against the Russians over Cuba.

The Cuban Missile Crisis

What You Should Know

The island of Cuba is only 90 miles from the Florida coast of the USA. Until 1959 it was strongly influenced by the USA which controlled and exploited most of Cuba's economy.

In 1959 a revolution led by Fidel Castro took over Cuba and he accepted Russian help to rebuild Cuba's economy. In exchange the Russians wanted to build missile bases in Cuba.

Most of mainland USA would be under threat from Russian missiles for the very first time.

When American spy planes photographed Russian missiles on Cuba, President Kennedy ordered their withdrawal but the Russians refused. Some American Generals wanted to invade Cuba even if it meant a new world war.

Instead, Kennedy ordered a blockade of Cuba which meant no supply ships could go into or out of Cuba without US approval. The crisis ended when the Russians agreed to dismantle the missile sites. The world had come very close to a Third World War as a result of superpower rivalry.

You must be able to describe the events known as the Cuban Missile Crisis and explain fully why such superpower rivalry was of such a concern to the rest of the world.

Questions and Answers

The Cuban Missile Crisis – General

Source A is about the Cuban missile crisis of 1962:

'When it became clear that the Russians were preparing to use Cuba as an important missile base President Kennedy could not ignore the threat only 90 miles from the American coast. The placing of these weapons of mass destruction so close to the USA was a threat to the safety and security of all Americans and could not be tolerated.'

KU Q Why was the USA worried about Russian involvement in Cuba?

Questions and Answers continued

KU

From the source:

- The Russians were preparing to use Cuba as an important missile base.
- These bases were only 90 miles from the American coast.
- The missiles threatened the safety and security of all Americans.

From recall:

- Russia and America were rivals and enemies in the Cold War.
- It was the first time the homeland of the USA had been under direct threat from Russia.
- Cuba had become a communist country after the revolution. It was the first communist base in the western hemisphere.
- Neither side could afford to back down in the tension of the Cold War.

ES Q *Source B* gives information about the importance of the Cuban crisis:

> **The Cuban crisis emphasised the importance of the superpowers. Britain still had no real influence on the use of nuclear weapons. Yet America had bases in Britain which would have been among the first targets of a Soviet nuclear strike.**

How fully does *Source B* describe international relations in the 1960s?

ES

The source mentions:

- The Cuban Crisis but it does not explain why there was a crisis.
- The superpowers and the relative unimportance of Britain.
- That the USA had nuclear weapons based in Britain.
- It suggests that Britain was an ally of America and that Russia was an enemy of Britain and France.
- It suggests that tension was high between the superpowers with the possibility of a first strike against Britain.
- The source does not deal with the entire 1960s, for example, there is no mention of the crisis over Berlin or superpower involvement in the Vietnam war or the Space Race.
- There is no mention of peaceful competitive coexistence which developed in the 1960s.

Chapter 6

UNIT 3 CONTEXT C: RUSSIA 1914–1941

 The Tsarist State

What You Should Know

In 1914 the huge Russian Empire was ruled by Tsar Nicholas II. Although there was a parliament called a Duma it had little power. Russia was an autocracy which meant the Tsar had total power and he was against any change.

 You should be able to describe the Tsarist system of government and be able to use the word autocracy and autocratic.

What You Should Know

Ordinary Russians suffered from high taxes, high rents and low wages. Discontent grew with the corrupt and inefficient way that Russia was governed and the terrible living and working conditions faced by most Russians.

 You should be able to describe the harsh living and working conditions of Russians in both towns and the countryside.

What You Should Know

There was some opposition to the Tsarist system of government. Groups such as the Kadets, the Social Revolutionaries and the Social Democrats wanted change but any opposition risked discovery by the secret police called the Okrhana. However, the bulk of the people supported the Tsar and still thought of him as 'The Little Father', given to them by God to rule them.

! You must also be prepared to explain why there was some opposition to the Tsarist government and also describe what the different opposition groups wanted. You should also be aware of the split in the Social Revolutionaries into Bolshevik and Menshevik, what those two groups wanted and how they could best achieve their aims.

Questions *and* Answers

The Tsarist State – General

Source A gives evidence about the government of Russia before the First World War:

> In the Russian system of government the Tsar had absolute power over his people. The autocracy depended on three powerful groups – the nobility, the church and the army. They in turn depended on the Tsar for their power, their wealth and their privileges.

KU Q Describe the system of government in Russia before 1917

KU

From the source:

◆ The Tsar had absolute power.

◆ The system of government depended on three groups – the nobility, the church and the army.

◆ These groups depended on the Tsar for their power.

From your own knowledge you could mention:

◆ There was no democracy.

◆ The Tsar also depended on the secret police.

◆ Ordinary people had no power or influence.

◆ The system was called an autocracy.

◆ Dumas – or parliaments – existed in the years before the First World War.

Questions and Answers continued

ES Q   *Source B* is by historian Martin Roberts and is about Tsar Nicholas II:

'Nicholas was not stupid but he lacked confidence in his abilities as a ruler. He was no judge of the right men to be ministers and relied too much on his strong willed but foolish wife, Alexandra. She told her husband that the Russian people needed to feel an iron hand. She also told him he was the lord and master of Russia, placed there by God Almighty.'

Source C comes from 'The Empire of the Tsar' by Tony Howarth.

'Nicholas II became Tsar in 1894. He was absolute ruler of the Empire and governed through a corrupt civil service. Opposition was dealt with by the secret police, the army and the Cossacks. The Orthodox Church taught respect for the Tsar.'

To what extent do *Sources B* and *C* give an accurate picture of the Russian monarchy at the time of Nicholas II? You should use your own knowledge and give reasons for your answer.

ES

Together the sources give a fairly accurate impression of the Russian monarchy. The Tsar was an absolute ruler (*Source B*), 'placed there by God almighty (*Source B*). He was influenced strongly by his wife (*Source B*) and the Tsar did rely on repression through the secret police and Cossacks to maintain control (*Source C*).

Neither source mentions some changes that took place as a result of the October Manifesto such as the Duma. (Since the question asks you to use your own knowledge you can either explain more fully points made in the source or bring in new information.)

Russia in the First World War

What You Should Know

In August 1914 Russia entered the First World War.

The Russian army had poor leadership while its soldiers were poorly trained and equipped. In 1915 the Tsar took personal control of the army. This was a mistake since all of Russia's problems in the war could be blamed on him.

What you should know continued ➤

What You Should Know continued

Away from the fighting, food and fuel shortages in the cities increased discontent with the Tsar. The hardship and suffering caused by the war eventually led to the collapse of the Tsarist system of government.

By the winter of 1916/17 the Russian army was facing defeat and in the cities, especially St Petersburg, bread queues increased and the people became angrier.

Support for the Tsar was vanishing.

You must be able to describe fully the problems faced by the Russian army and civilians in the cities as the war dragged on.

You should also be able to explain why the war increased discontent with the Tsar.

What You Should Know

Confidence in the Tsar fell when it was discovered that a mysterious monk called Rasputin had influence over the Tsar's wife Alexandra, so much so that Rasputin was almost controlling the Russian government while the Tsar was away with his armies. Not only that, the Tsar's wife Alexandra was a German and some Russians thought she was a spy.

Be prepared to describe and explain the influence of Rasputin.

Questions and Answers

Russia in the First World War – Credit

'There was evidence of widespread discontent with the Tsar's government by the end of 1916.'

KU Q Why were so many Russians discontented with the Tsar's government by late 1916?

Questions *and* Answers *continued* ?

KU

You should mention in your answer most of the following:

◆ Disappointment and defeat.

◆ Worry about conditions at the front and at home.

◆ The Tsar took personal responsibility when he became commander in chief.

◆ People were worried and shocked by the influence of Rasputin over the government.

ES Q *Source A* is taken from 'The End of the Russian Empire' by M. Florinsky.

'At the beginning of January 1917, General Krimov arrived from the front and asked to be given an opportunity to inform the members of the Duma about the disastrous conditions at the front and the spirit of the army. He said: "There can be no hope of victory until the Government has changed its course to one the army could trust. The spirit of the army is such that the news of the overthrow of the Government would be welcomed with joy. A revolution is coming soon."'

How fully does *Source A* explain discontent within the Russian army by early 1917?

ES

It is often wise to write that a source partly explains a situation. That lets you mention what *is* and *is not* in the source:

◆ The soldiers did not believe the policies of the government would be successful.

◆ There was almost no hope of victory.

◆ The soldiers wanted a new government.

However, the source does **not** mention:

◆ Lack of supplies, weapons or ammunition.

◆ Concern about families back home.

◆ The continuing offensives in the war leading to huge casualty rates.

◆ The feeling that the army was being betrayed by the Tsarina and, earlier, Rasputin.

The October Revolution

What You Should Know

The Provisional Government ruled Russia from February to October 1917 but was eventually overthrown by a revolution organised by the Bolsheviks.

Discontent with the Provisional Government increased through 1917. When Lenin returned to Russia he declared that there should be no co-operation between the soviet and the Provisional Government and he made promises of peace, bread, land and freedom if the people supported the Bolsheviks.

Between 24 and 26 October the Bolshevik Revolution overthrew the Provisional Government.

 You must also be able to explain why discontent with the Provisional Government grew during the summer of 1917.

Remember

You should be able to describe the events of the July Days and the Kornilov revolt.

You should also be able to explain why these events are connected to the changing fortunes of the Bolsheviks in 1917.

 You must be able to describe the events of the October revolution and explain why the Bolsheviks were successful (that also includes reasons why the provisional Government had lost so much support).

Questions and Answers

The October Revolution – Credit

Within six months Lenin was urging that the time was right for the Bolsheviks to seize power.

KU Q Explain why, by October 1917, Lenin thought the time was right for the Bolsheviks to seize power.

Questions *and* Answers *continued* (?)

KU

- The population was discontented by the continuing war.

- Food shortages were increasing in the cities.

- Fuel shortages were increasing in the cities.

- The Soviets were under Bolshevik control.

- The Bolsheviks had appeared patriotic saviours of the Government during and after the Kornilov Revolt.

- The Bolsheviks were armed during the Kornilov revolt and still had the weapons!

ES Q The following source is about the Provisional Government.

Source A is from a speech by Lenin in April 1917.

Do not believe the promises of the Provisional Government. They are deceiving you and the whole Russian people. The people need peace; the people need bread; the people need land. And they give you war, hunger, no bread and leave the landlords still on the land. We must fight for the social revolution.

Discuss Lenin's views about the Provisional Government.

ES

- Lenin told the people not to believe the promises of the Provisional Government.

- Lenin considered the policies of the Provisional Government to be wrong.

- The Provisional Government was the main 'competition' to Lenin so he was inevitably against them and wanted others to feel the same.

- Lenin needed to be listened to and increase his support.

- He had to be different from the Provisional Government.

- He felt the Provisional Government had failed to deliver what the Russian people wanted – peace, bread and land.

The Bolshevik State

What You Should Know

After the October Revolution Russia was ruled by the Bolsheviks. Lenin, leader of the Bolsheviks, believed the revolution had to be followed by a 'dictatorship of the proletariat', which really meant destroying any opposition. A new secret police was created called the Cheka and they began a policy called 'Red Terror' against anyone who disagreed with the Bolsheviks.

You should be able to use accurately and appropriately the word Cheka and the phrase Red Terror.

You must also be able to explain why the Red Terror was started and describe some of the methods of the Bolsheviks in enforcing their authority.

What You Should Know

Lenin ended the war by surrendering to Germany and he introduced several reforms.

When elections to the Constituent Assembly were held the Bolsheviks lost, so Lenin used his Red Guards to close down the Assembly.

By the summer of 1918 the Bolsheviks had banned all other political parties.

In March 1917 Lenin agreed to the Treaty of Brest-Litovsk which formally ended the war against Germany. Russia lost huge amounts of land, resources and money.

Key Points

Describe the reforms that Lenin introduced and explain how they would make life in Russia better.

You should be able to explain why the results of the elections for the Constituent Assembly made Lenin change his mind about political freedom.

Questions and Answers

The Bolshevik State – General

In *Source A* Felix Dzerzhipsky describes the role of the Cheka (Secret Police) in July 1918:

'The Cheka is not a court. The Cheka is the defence of the revolution just as the Red Army is. As in the Civil War the Red Army cannot stop to ask whether it may harm particular individuals but must concentrate on one thing, so the Cheka must defend the revolution and conquer the enemy even if its sword falls occasionally on the heads of the innocent.'

KU Q According to *Source A*, what was the purpose of the Cheka?

KU

From the source:

◆ It is not a court but must act quickly against enemies of the Bolsheviks.

◆ The purpose of the Cheka was to defend the revolution and to conquer the enemy.

From your own knowledge:

◆ The Cheka spied on enemies.

◆ It created fear among the enemies of the Bolsheviks.

◆ It also maintained loyalty among the Bolsheviks as people were afraid of the Cheka accusing them of a crime.

ES Q *Source B* is from a letter written in 1919 by Gorky, a Bolshevik supporter, about the Red Terror:

'In my view the arrests of good Bolsheviks by the Cheka cannot be justified. The disgusting crimes the Red Terror carried out in Petersburg during the past few weeks have brought shame to the Government and aroused universal hatred for its treatment of the people. All these arrests I see as the deliberate destruction of the best brains of the country and I declare that the actions of the Cheka has turned me into an enemy of the Government.'

How useful is *Source B* as evidence about the effects of the Terror on Russia?

Questions *and* **Answers** *continued*

ES

The letter shows that even some Bolsheviks were opposed to the Red Terror.

It is a primary source, relevant to the topic and provides eye witness opinions.

Gorky believes the arrests cannot be justified. He believes the Red Terror has hurt the international image of the revolution and 'brought shame to the Government and aroused universal hatred'.

Gorky is taking a huge personal risk by writing the letter telling how he felt.

He claims the Red Terror has turned him against the Government.

You should therefore conclude that the source is useful as evidence but only when seen as written by someone who now thinks of himself as an enemy, so his version of events will be biased against the Red Terror, the Cheka and the Bolshevik Government.

The Civil War

What You Should Know

The Russian civil war broke out in 1918 and the fighting continued until 1922. Groups who were opposed to Lenin and the Bolsheviks began to gather armies to fight. These 'White' forces were against the Bolsheviks who were known as the 'Reds'. The Whites were supported by Russia's former allies Britain and France who wanted to keep Russia in the war. The Red Army was led by Trotsky and he knew that for the Bolsheviks to win two things were needed. The Red army must be kept loyal and the troops must be kept supplied with food, weapons and equipment.

 You must be able to explain fully why the Whites lost the civil war and why the Reds won.

What You Should Know

During the Civil War Lenin made big changes to the Russian economy. His policy was called War Communism and in order to keep the Red Army supplied with food it meant government control of all parts of the economy.

What you should know continued ➤

> **What You Should Know** *continued* ✔
>
> You must be able to describe how War Communism operated and also explain why it became hugely unpopular and the problems it led to.
>
> You should also be able to explain why events at the Kronstadt naval base convinced Lenin that another change was necessary.
>
> In 1922, as the civil war ended and the Bolshevik state had survived, Lenin introduced a new policy called the New Economic Policy (NEP).
>
> You must be able to explain why the New Economic Policy was introduced and describe how it operated.

Questions *and* Answers

The Civil War – Credit

> When the Bolsheviks seized power in October 1917, they found a country on the verge of economic collapse.

KU Q Describe fully the Bolshevik Government's actions and their effects during the period of

EITHER

(a) War Communism

OR

(b) the New Economic Policy

(For this answer you should write a short essay of several paragraphs.)

KU

You would be expected to mention the following in your answer:

a) War Communism

War Communism created social discontent and led to riots, strikes and demonstations. War Communism tried to impose Communist ideology on farming and on industry. Lenin feared counter revolution so needed to guarantee food supplies to the cities and the Red Army in order to win the civil war.

Questions *and* Answers *continued*

Land was taken over by the Bolsheviks. It became illegal to employ people or work and sell anything for a profit.

Red Army squads went into the country to seize food supplies from villages.

A huge famine swept over Russia caused by War Communism.

At the Kronstadt naval base Bolshevik sailors and soliders mutinied and said they would not accept Bolshevik orders until War Communism was stopped.

War Communism stopped in March 1921.

(b) the New Economic Policy

The NEP was introduced to cure the problems created by War Communism and stop the wave of discontent with Bolshevik rule.

Farmers were allowed to sell surplus food for a profit once again.

Workers could be employed again and paid wages.

Farmers who prospered and employed other workers were called *kulaks*.

The NEP encouraged trade again, opened state banks and allowed factories employing less than twenty people to be given back to their previous owners.

The NEP benefited the peasants and improved food production in Russia. The people were given incentives to work harder which had been taken away under War Communism.

NEP was stopped by Stalin in January 1929.

ES Q *Source A* is from a leaflet distributed by the Bolsheviks to Allied troops invading Russia in 1919:

'For the first time in history the working people have control of their country. The workers of all countries are striving to achieve this. We in Russia have succeeded. We have thrown off the rule of the Tsar, of landlords and of capitalists. But we still have tremendous difficulties to overcome. We cannot build a new society in a day. We deserve to be left alone. We ask you, are you going to crush us? To help give Russia back to the landlords, the capitalists and the Tsar?'

What is the attitude shown in *Source A* towards the situation in Russia in 1919?

Questions and Answers continued

ES

The attitude is that Russia was the first country in the world in which the working people had control of the country.

Other workers elsewhere would like to achieve that.

The writer wanted Russia to be left alone to consolidate the gains made.

The writer knew there was much work to be done within Russia.

The writer is trying to persuade Allied soliders that they should not fight the new Bolshevik State, especially since their victory would only turn the clock back to the old days of the Tsar.

The writer implies such an allied victory would not help the ordinary soldiers so why should they fight against the workers' state?

Stalin

Be able to explain why Lenin did not want Stalin to succeed him. You must then be able to describe how Stalin managed to become all powerful in Russia.

What You Should Know

When Lenin died in 1924 there were two main rivals for the leadership of the party, Leon Trotsky and Joseph Stalin. By 1928 Stalin was leader and Trotsky was thrown out of the Bolshevik party.

Stalin aimed to do three things:

Firstly Stalin wanted to modernise Russia and he introduced Five Year Plans to achieve production standards. There were huge increases in the production of coal, oil, steel and electricity and transport.

Secondly Stalin modernised agriculture by introducing collectivisation. Peasants and wealthier farmers called Kulaks were crushed by Stalin.

You must be able to explain the reasons for collectivisation and the Five Year Plans and also describe fully the effects of those policies.

What you should know continued ➤

HOW TO PASS STANDARD GRADE HISTORY

> ### *What You Should Know continued*
>
> *Thirdly* Stalin focused on destroying any threat to him.
>
> Between 1934 and 1938 Stalin's 'purges' killed or imprisoned anyone who opposed him or his polices.
>
> **Be able to explain the phrase 'show trials' and why Stalin felt the need to carry out his purges.**

Questions and Answers

Stalin – General

Source A is from a recent book about collectivisation:

The Kulaks hated Stalin's plan for collectivisation. Rather than accept the new rules many farmers ate all their seeds and animals rather than see them taken away and given to collective farms. Anything not used up was hidden from the Requisition Squads sent to grab the farmers possessions. Some Commissars sent to enforce collectivisation were murdered as they tried to impose the new policies.

KU Q   How did many farmers react to the new plans for collectivisation?
(6 marks)

KU

From the source:

◆ Farmers ate seeds and killed their animals rather than give them to the collectives.

◆ Some Commissars were murdered.

◆ Anything not used up by the farmers was hidden so that government Requisition Squads could not get it.

From your own knowledge:

◆ Kulaks burned their crops to prevent the government taking them.

◆ Peasants destroyed equipment to prevent the collectives using them.

◆ Some Kulaks organised armed resistance and fought requisition squads.

◆ Many Kulaks left Russia rather than join the collectives.

◆ There was some sabotage of new equipment and machinery belonging to the collective farms.

Questions and **Answers** continued

ES Q *Source B is from Stalin's speech to the Party Congress in 1927.*

The way to improve agriculture is to turn the small and scattered peasant farms into large united farms based on the common cultivation of the land. The way ahead is to unite the small peasant farms gradually but surely, not by pressure but by example and persuasion, into large farms based on common, co-operative collective cultivation of the land. There is no other way to improve.

Discuss Stalin's attitude towards agricultural change in Russia.

ES

Improvements were needed. Stalin knew he needed efficient food production to feed the industrial workers needed for his Five Year Plan industrialisation programmes.

Stalin needed to keep the farms loyal to the revolution and he saw the Kulaks as a threat to his control, influence and ideas.

Stalin wanted to improve farming.

He described his changes as 'the way ahead'.

He claimed not to want to force change but to persuade changes to happen.

He did not see an alternative to his ideas. 'There is no other way'.

He wanted collectivisation – 'common, co-operative collective cultivation of the land.'

UNIT 3 CONTEXT D: GERMANY 1918–1939

Germany in 1918

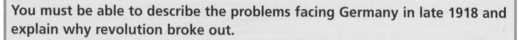

What You Should Know

After fighting for four years, by the autumn of 1918 it was obvious that Germany was about to lose the First World War. The German army was defeated, its allies had surrendered and inside Germany the civilian population was facing serious hardships.

In November 1918 revolution spread across Germany. Soldiers, sailors and civilians wanted the war to end and the Kaiser abdicated on 9 November 1918.

You must be able to describe the problems facing Germany in late 1918 and explain why revolution broke out.

You should also be able to use the words monarchy, revolution, abdicate and republic in answers on this section.

What You Should Know

When the Kaiser abdicated a new Provisional Government was created led by Friedrich Ebert, leader of the Social Democratic Party (SPD). Ebert knew there was a danger of Communist revolution sweeping over Germany and in 1919 the Spartacists, who later became known as the Communist Party or KPD, tried to start a revolution to create a new Communist Germany. The attempted revolution failed. Ebert had help from the army and groups of ex soldiers called Freikorps who used extreme brutality to destroy the revolutionaries.

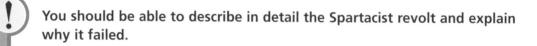

You should be able to describe in detail the Spartacist revolt and explain why it failed.

Questions *and* Answers

Germany in 1918 – General

Source A is a description of problems faced by the German army in late 1918:

The German army was retreating. All along the front line German soldiers are found hiding in shell holes and ruined buildings. They offer no resistance but surrender at once. Batches of prisoners are being brought back in a steady stream. Many say they are fed up with the war.

KU Q Describe the problems faced by the German army in 1918.
(5 marks)

KU

From the source:

◆ The army was being pushed back (retreating).

◆ Soldiers were surrendering.

◆ Many German prisoners were being taken.

◆ Soldiers were fed up with the war.

From your own knowledge:

◆ Germany's allies surrendered.

◆ The arrival of USA soldiers in large numbers ended German hopes of victory.

◆ The British naval blockade caused military shortages.

ES Q Jan Valtin, a sailor in November 1918 wrote:

'That night I saw the mutinous sailors roll in to Bremen with red flags (the symbol of revolution) and machine guns mounted on the trucks. Many of the workers were armed with guns. A frightened old woman wailed "What is the world coming to?" A young worker grasped the old woman's shoulders. He laughed and said "Revolution, Madam."...'

Why is *Source B* valuable evidence about Germany at the end of the war?

Questions *and* Answers *continued*

ES

You should mention it is a primary source from an eye witness to events at end of war.

◆ It mentions that sailors mutinied which was the start of the revolution.

◆ It reports the claim of the workers that they wanted revolution.

◆ It locates the events in Bremen.

The Weimar Constitution

What You Should Know

The title 'Weimar Germany' or 'The Weimar Republic' refers to a time between 1919 and 1933 when Germany was a Republic ruled by elected representatives. The new democratic republic created a constitution which tried to be fair to everyone but it had serious weaknesses.

Remember

You must be able to describe ways in which the new constitution tried to be fair.

You must also be able to describe some of the political weaknesses of the new constitution.

Questions *and* Answers

The Weimar Constitution – Credit

The new constitution tried to be fair to everyone but it had serious weaknesses.

KU Q Describe how the new constitution tried to be fair to everyone.

Questions *and* Answers *continued*

KU

This question could be worth 8 or, more likely, 4 marks. *The amount of detail you should include depends on the number of marks.*

Your answer should mention most of the following:

◆ All Germans were equal before the law.

◆ All phone calls and letters were private and could not be opened by the authorities.

◆ The authorities could not enter private houses without search warrants.

◆ All Germans over 20 could vote.

◆ All Germans had freedom of speech and could write their opinions freely.

◆ Germans could join any legal organisation or group they wanted to.

◆ A voting system based on proportional representation meant that everyone's political choice had a fair chance of being represented in the Reichstag.

ES Q *Source A* is from the diary of a German army officer writing in 1919:

'Democracy! There was no democracy when Germany was great under the Kaiser. Now Germany's leaders must listen to the voice of every shop keeper and farm labourer, along with their women. The backbone of Germany is its landowners and its army officers. They alone should have power!'

What is the attitude of the ex army officer in *Source A* to the new democratic government?

ES

◆ The writer of *Source A* does not like the new democratic government.

◆ He believed that Germany was better off under the Kaiser.

◆ He believed the true ruling class should be landowners and its army officers.

◆ He resents having to consider the opinions of 'every shop keeper and farm labourer, along with their women.'

◆ Political power should be restricted to a ruling elite.

◆ The writer dislikes democracy as a political idea.

Figure 7.1 Germany in 1918

The Treaty of Versailles

What You Should Know

On 28 June 1919 the Treaty of Versailles officially ended the First World War. Most Germans were left with a desire for revenge, an important factor used by Hitler in his rise to power several years later.

You must be able to describe how Germany was affected by the treaty and also explain why Germany felt so angry about it.

Questions and Answers

The Treaty of Versailles – General
(for Credit questions about Versailles see Unit 2 Context B)

> The peace treaty caused outrage in Germany and prepared the way for future trouble.

KU Q For what reasons did Germans dislike the Treaty of Versailles?
(6 marks)

> KU
>
> It was a dictated treaty – not based on Wilson's 14 Points.
>
> Germany had to accept War Guilt.
>
> Germany lost land, resources, population and its armed forces.
>
> Germany was made to sign under threat of invasion.
>
> Germany felt humiliated.

Questions *and* Answers *continued* **(?)**

ES Q *Source A* was written by a British woman who had married a German nobleman and who was living in Germany when the treaty was signed:

'People were ready here to make reparation for the wrong done by their leaders, but now they say that Wilson has broken his word and an undying hate is in the heart of every German. Over and over again I hear the same words, "We shall hate our conquerors with a hatred that will only cease when the day of our revenge comes again".'

Source B was written by Toni Sender, a German woman, in 1919:

'What could we do? What was the alternative of not signing? The German people wanted peace, they were exhausted. Not to sign would mean occupation of the most important territories, the blockade continued, unemployment, hunger, the death of thousands, the holding back of our war prisoners – a catastrophe which would force us to sign more humiliating conditions.'

Compare the attitudes towards the Treaty in *Sources A* and *B*.

ES

◆ *A* wants revenge but *B* is accepting the treaty.

◆ *A* believes Germany was tricked into accepting the treaty but *B* believes there was no choice.

◆ *A* speaks about undying hatred to the peacemakers at Versailles whereas *B* believes it was the best option.

◆ *A* looks to the future and is rather unrealistic but *B* is realistic pointing out the problems which Germany had which led to defeat.

Figure 7.2 The Treaty of Versailles – Clemenceau the Vampire in Germany 1918

The Ruhr and Hyperinflation

What You Should Know

In 1923 French and Belgian troops invaded the Ruhr area of Germany to force Germany to pay reparations on time. As a result of the invasion Germany's economy collapsed and hyperinflation struck Germany. German money lost its value. Once again Germans blamed their own government for being weak and powerless. The German economy only recovered thanks to American loans of money.

You should be able to explain why the economic crisis of 1923 happened and also describe the effects of hyperinflation on Germany.

Questions *and* Answers

The Ruhr and Hyperinflation – General

> *Source A* is from a recent school book about Germany in the 1920s:

'France and Belgium wanted to force Germany to pay reparations. Their troops occupied the Ruhr region in western Germany. The Ruhr was Germany's industrial heart which produced 80 per cent of its steel and 71 per cent of its coal production. France intended to force Germany to pay up or work under French control.'

KU Q Explain why French and Belgian troops invaded the Ruhr in 1923.
(6 marks)

KU

From the source:

◆ France and Belgium wanted to force Germany to pay reparations.

◆ The Ruhr was Germany's industrial heart which produced 80 per cent of its steel and 71 per cent of its coal

◆ France and Belgium wanted Germans in the Ruhr to work under French control.

From your own knowledge:

◆ Germany had failed to pay up reparations on time.

◆ The Ruhr produced Germany's wealth.

◆ France and Belgium wanted to keep Germany weak.

Questions *and* Answers *continued*

ES Q *Source A* is from an interview with a woman who lived through the hyperinflation crisis:

'As soon as I received my salary I rushed out to buy the daily necessities. My daily salary, as editor of a magazine, was just enough to buy one loaf of bread and a small piece of cheese or some oatmeal. On one occasion a private lesson I gave was paid somewhat better – by one loaf of bread for the hour.'

How useful is *Source A* for finding out about the effects of hyperinflation on the German people?

ES

The woman gives first hand evidence, it is a primary source.

It gives details of what the woman's salary could buy.

It shows that people were happier if they were paid in something they could use or eat rather than worthless paper money.

But the source only gives one person's memory. It does not tell us anything about other problems such as starvation and homelessness which affected many Germans.

The Munich Putsch

What You Should Know

In November 1923 the Nazis tried to seize power in Munich. The Nazi leader, Adolf Hitler, intended to overthrow the Weimar Republic.

The putsch failed but the trial got big publicity. While in prison Hitler decided the Nazis would campaign in future to achieve power legally.

You should be able to describe the main events of the Munich Putsch and also be able to explain two main things – why it happened and what the consequences of the putsch were for Hitler and for democracy in Germany.

Questions and Answers

The Munich Putsch – Credit

The Munich Putsch was an important first step for the Nazis.

KU Q What were the consequences of the Munich Putsch for Hitler and for Germany?

KU

You should mention the following:

- The putsch and the trial gained the Nazis national publicity.
- Hitler was only given a short prison sentence – an indication that powerful people sympathised with the Nazis which suggested these people were not supporters of democracy.
- Hitler decided to change Nazi party tactics and work towards winning elections.
- In prison Hitler wrote *Mein Kampf*.

ES Q *Source A was written by a German in 1936:*

'At about noon a procession of 2000 National Socialists marched, twelve abreast, through Munich. At the first shot Hitler had flung himself to the ground. He injured his arm, but this did not prevent him from running. He found his car and drove into the mountains. After the Putsch Hitler wanted "to make himself scarce". This simply meant run away and hide.'

Source B is from the official biography of Adolf Hitler published by the Nazi Party in 1934:

'As they marched through Munich Hitler shouted, "Close the ranks," and linked arms with his neighbours. The body of the man with whom Hitler was linked shot up into the air like a ball then fell to the ground. Hitler picked him up and carried him on his shoulders. "If I can only get him to the car," Hitler thought, "then the boy is saved".'

To what extent do *Sources A* and *B* agree about Hitler's actions during the Munich Putsch?

Questions and Answers continued

ES

Both sources agree that Hitler marched through Munich in ranks with other people.

They agree that shots were fired.

The sources then disagree. *Source A* suggests that Hitler behaved in a cowardly way while *B* tried to show Hitler as a hero.

Source A says Hitler 'flung himself to the ground' when the first shots were fired but *B* states that Hitler tried to save a wounded boy.

Source A says that Hitler ran away while *B* suggests Hitler tried to pick up the wounded boy and take him to safety. *Source A* says Hitler hurt his arm when he fell but *B* says his arm was hurt because it was twisted by his falling comrade.

Hitler Becomes Chancellor

What You Should Know

By 1932 the Nazis became the biggest political party in the Reichstag.

The Nazis were helped by important businessmen and some Weimar politicians who thought the Nazis could be useful to them. In January 1933 Hitler became Chancellor of Germany.

You must be able to describe how the Nazis increased their political power after 1930 and also explain why it is NOT correct to say that Hitler achieved total power in January 1933.

Questions and Answers

Hitler Becomes Chancellor – Credit

KU Q Describe what happened in German politics between 1929 and 1933 which led to Hitler becoming Chancellor.

For this answer you should write a short essay of several paragraphs.

Questions and Answers continued

KU

In your answer you should mention:

◆ The Nazis gained support from Alfred Hugenberg who owned most of Germany's new cinema industry and hundreds of local newspapers.

◆ The Nazis gained financial support from big business.

◆ Between 1930 and 1932 the democratic parties could not agree on how to deal with Germany's problems.

◆ In the spring of 1930 Heinrich Bruning became Chancellor. He ruled Germany without majority support in the Reichstag.

◆ In 1932 Franz von Papen replaced Bruning as Chancellor. He suggested 'the constitution should be ignored for the sake of the country.'

◆ Von Papen realised the Nazis could be useful to his political ambitions.

◆ Von Papen offered Hitler the job of Vice Chancellor but Hitler refused.

◆ Von Papen then persuaded Hindenburg to appoint Adolf Hitler as Chancellor and on 30 January 1933 Adolf Hitler became Chancellor of the Weimar Republic.

ES Q *Source A is an election poster in 1932. The words on it say, 'Hitler, our last hope'.*

How fully does this poster explain the reasons why Hitler became Chancellor?

ES

The poster suggests Hitler had answers to Germany's problems.

The poster suggests the Nazis were the last and only hope for people who were disillusioned by the other political parties.

The expression on the faces suggest the people were desperate for answers.

However, the poster tells us nothing of how the Nazis were helped by important businessmen and some Weimar politicians who thought the Nazis could be useful to them.

Figure 7.3 Source A: Hitler becomes Chancellor

The Road to Dictatorship

What You Should Know

When Hitler became Chancellor in January 1933 there were only three other Nazis in the coalition government.

On 27 February 1933, only one week before the next election, the Reichstag was burned down. Hitler claimed it was part of a Communist plot to start a revolution. To deal with that threat an Enabling Act gave Hitler so much power he was almost a dictator.

Between 1933 and 1934 Hitler removed the last remains of democracy in Germany. He also got rid of possible challenges to his power where he destroyed the power of the SA in the Night of the Long Knives. When President Hindenburg died, Hitler made himself supreme ruler of Germany.

Key Points

◆ **You should be able to describe what Hitler did to turn himself from Chancellor of Germany into the Dictator of Germany.**

◆ **You should also be able to explain why the Reichstag fire, the Enabling Act and the Night of the Long Knives were important to Hitler and for democracy in Germany.**

HOW TO PASS STANDARD GRADE HISTORY

Questions *and* Answers

The Road to Dictatorship – General

Source A is what Hitler is reported to have said when he heard about the Reichstag fire:

'There will be no mercy now. Anyone who stands in our way will be cut down. Every Communist official should be shot where he is found. Everybody supporting the Communists must be arrested. The Communist Party should have no rights in Germany.'

KU Q What did Hitler want to happen to the Communists after the Reichstag fire? *(4 marks)*

> **KU**
>
> From the source:
> ◆ Communists should be shot.
> ◆ Communist supporters must be arrested.
> ◆ Communist Party should have no rights in Germany.
>
> From your own knowledge:
> ◆ He wanted them to lose the election.
> ◆ Communist newspapers were banned.
> ◆ Communist meetings were stopped.
> ◆ Eventually the Communist Party was to be banned.

ES Q *Source B* is from a recent school book about the Enabling Act of March 1933:

'The new law took away the basic rights of the German people. Newspapers could be censored and the right of members of the public to attend meetings was limited. Even private letters and phone calls could be checked. Newspapers belonging to the political opponents of the Nazis were closed down in the run up to the elections. The Nazis were triumphant.'

Explain how the Enabling Act ended democracy in Germany.

Questions and **Answers** continued

ES

You should mention:

◆ Newspapers were censored.

◆ The right to attend meetings was limited.

◆ Private letters and phone calls were intercepted and checked.

◆ The basic rights of the German people were taken away.

◆ Opposition newspapers were closed down.

◆ The basic rights of the fundamental laws were taken away.

In this answer you should also show that you understand what democracy was and how it was ended by the new Nazi laws. You could mention points such as:

◆ The Nazis moved towards dictatorship.

◆ Free choice was ended.

◆ Personal freedoms were restricted.

◆ People could be taken away and kept in prison without charge or trial.

◆ Opposition political parties were banned.

Life in Nazi Germany

The Persecution of the Jews

What You Should Know

At first Nazi policy was aimed at persuading Jews to leave Germany but between 1933 and 1939 persecution of Jews got worse. Persecution means picking on a people, bullying them and in the case of the Nazis, eventually murdering Jews. Eventually the racist policies of the Nazis led to the 'Final Solution' of the Jewish 'problem' – the mass murder of Jews which is known today as the Holocaust.

You must be able to describe the various ways Jews were persecuted by the Nazis.

Questions and Answers

The Persecution of the Jews – Credit

> Jews in Germany were persecuted as soon as the Nazis came to power.

KU Q Describe the ways in which Jews were persecuted by the Nazis.
(6 marks)

KU

You should mention the following examples of ways in which Jews were persecuted by the Nazis:

◆ Jewish shops were boycotted.

◆ Laws, such as the Nuremberg Laws to protect 'Blood and Honour', discriminated against Jews.

◆ Segregation of Jews.

◆ Bullying and intimidation.

◆ Jews not allowed to marry non-Jewish Germans.

◆ Kristallnacht.

◆ Jews were expelled from Germany.

◆ Anti-semitic propaganda was used all over Germany.

Youth in Nazi Germany

What You Should Know

The Nazis wanted to indoctrinate the youth of Germany. In schools, young Germans were taught to be good Nazis.

Out of school, youth organisations such as the Hitler Youth and the League of German Maidens continued the work of turning Germany's youth into supporters of Hitler and the Nazis. Boys were trained for military service while the focus of girls' education was to turn them into good mothers of the future master race.

You should be able to describe the ways in which Nazi education and youth groups tried to indoctrinate the youth of Germany.

Questions *and* Answers *continued*

Youth in Nazi Germany – General

ES Q *Source A* is from a recent textbook describing some of the activities of the Hitler Youth.

Many young people were attracted by the exciting and interesting range of activities of the Youth movement. There were many outdoor events such as camping and hiking, as well as sports. Some enjoyed the military aspects of the Youth movement: the uniforms, the marching and the discipline. Other young people liked the music that was a frequent part of their military parades.

How fully does *Source A* describe the ways Nazis attracted young people?

ES

From the source:

◆ Young people were attracted by the exciting and interesting range of activities.

◆ There were outdoor events such as hiking, camping, sports.

◆ Some people enjoyed military training activities and wearing uniforms.

◆ Some liked the music and parades.

From your own knowledge:

◆ It gave the children status.

◆ Girls attracted by domestic 'training'.

◆ Some boys enjoyed the practice battles.

◆ It gave many young Germans a sense of belonging.

The Nazi State – Keeping Control by Fear and Approval

What You Should Know

The Nazis used fear as a means of controlling the population. But be careful. Hitler did not terrorise the entire German population. Hitler knew he had to keep as many people as possible happy with the Nazi regime, or at least willing to accept it. One such organisation which provided leisure activities for German people was called Strength Through Joy.

You must be able to describe how the Nazis intimidated many people but also be able to explain why many German people actively supported the Nazi dictatorship.

Questions and **Answers**

The Nazi State – Keeping Control by Fear and Approval – Credit

ES Q Source A is from an interview with a member of the German Communist Party who was put in a concentration camp:

'I and other leaders of the Communist Party were ordered into a punishment room. It was only 60 cm by 60 cm. You could only stand upright in it – you couldn't sit or bend. I was in it for four days. I was repeatedly beaten. After four days my whole body was swollen from standing up.'

Source B is from a recent school text book about Germany in the 1930s:

'Each week Strength Through Joy organised leisure activities for workers such as theatre outings and hiking expeditions which were very popular at the time. Sports facilities were built and there was even the chance of a possible foreign holiday in Italy. In fact, Hitler even promised every German worker an affordable family car – a people's car – or in German, a Volkswagen!'

How fully do Sources A and B explain the ways in which the Nazis controlled the people of Germany in the 1930s?

ES

They show the contrast between the use of fear ('I was repeatedly beaten' – Source A) and the attempt by the Nazis to win acceptance by the German people by offering them the chance of a better life ('Hitler even promised every German worker an affordable family car' – Source B). Source B states that the activities were 'very popular' while Source A refers to 'punishment rooms'.

Source A indicates that fear and punishment were used against those who opposed the Nazis (Source A was written by a Communist) but for most people the chance of holidays, cars and leisure activities made Nazi Germany an attractive place to be.

However, the sources tell us nothing of the mass indoctrination, the use of propaganda, the control of media and education or the blocking of any voice against the Nazis, so the sources are only partly useful.

The Church in Nazi Germany and Opposition to the Nazis

What You Should Know

Hitler tried to control the Christian Churches in Germany. The Protestant Church became known as the Reich Church. Hitler made a Concordat, or agreement, with the Catholic Church but soon broke it. Hitler tried to replace Christianity with a new pagan form of worship. Some church priests, ministers and pastors accepted Nazi control but many others within the churches actively resisted the Nazis. One of the most famous opponents of the Nazis was Martin Niemoller.

 You should be able to describe the different ways the Nazis tried to deal with the Catholic and Protestant Churches.

Questions and Answers

The Church in Nazi Germany – General

> Source A is from a recent school text book:

'A Nazi organisation called German Christians replaced the Christian cross with the swastika as its symbol and the Bible was replaced by 'Mein Kampf' which was placed on the altar alongside a sword. On 17 December 1933 by the order of the Reich Bishop, the entire Protestant Youth Movement with more than 700,000 members was placed under the leadership of the Hitler Youth.'

KU Q Describe how the Nazis tried to control the Christian Church in Germany.

KU

From the source:

◆ A new organisation called the German Christians was created.

◆ The swastika replaced the cross on church altars.

◆ *Mein Kampf* replaced the Bible on church altars.

◆ A Reich Bishop was created.

◆ The Protestant Youth Movement became part of the Hitler Youth.

From your own knowledge:

◆ Concordat with Pope.

◆ Some church ministers and priests supported the Nazis especially since they persecuted Communists and Jews.

Opposition to the Nazis

What You Should Know

There were several reasons why opposition was difficult to organise and the opposition that did exist was small scale and based around various youth groups who did not want to conform to Nazi rules.

Be able to describe different types of resistance to the Nazis and explain why it was so difficult to organise large scale resistance to the Nazis.

Questions and Answers

Opposition to the Nazis – General

ES Q Explain the contrast between what Hitler is saying ('In these three years ...') and what the cartoon shows.

ES

Cartoonist often use irony. That means the images drawn often show the opposite to what the words mean. Do not think cartoonists believe what they make their characters say.

This cartoon shows various groups in Germany tied up and gagged with the word 'suppressed' on posters around their necks. Suppressed means their opinions have been censored or silenced. At the same time Hitler and his friends

Figure 7.4 In these three years I have restored honour and freedom to the German people.

are declaring that they have restored honour to the German people although their platform is supported by armed force. The cartoonist shows that there is little freedom in Nazi Germany despite what the words in the cartoon show.